MONEY
(How to flip the table off)

(for "occupy Wall Street ?)

Foreword

To act on the economy of a country, to go in the direction of progress, considered as a possibility of happiness, must be that country's leaders have the will and the means. Now currently most countries of the European Union, are paralyzed by the duty owed to the European treaties to give priority to the reduction of the budget deficit, which is still known as a brake on growth of progress. A series of important steps, suggested in the chapter "How to flip the table off" would change the situation, in other words would eliminate what in the economic system was led astray for decades for the benefit of financiers particularly attached to the decrease in expenses. Of course they are afraid not to have their money back. Growth in Europe is low or even reversed in some countries. Before proposing measures to revive economic activity, it will be necessary to return on the fundamentals that determine them, and on the logic of their operation. Among the main measures that I advocate, two are important: reconnect with Fordism (targeted small income) for growth, and establish two national currencies to control predatory financial flows.

The fundamental

Understand economy is to analyze the basic system that goes from production to consumption and, conversely, in a permanent cycle that dates back to the appearance of man on Earth. When homo erectus became homo sapiens, he developed tools to improve the performance of its work necessary for its survival. Then he invented a sophisticated tool, money, to assess the results of its work in order to easily exchange its products with those of its congeners. Some full of imagination have even begun to intervene in the process of production-consumption, with the concern to increase performance and some profit for themselves. Then it was the beginning of business wealth of countries by the markets. Capitalism is the result of accumulation of these profits. This trading system allowed everyone to enjoy reciprocal improvements.

The "homo aeconomicus" was born with its double aspect, a promise of wealth under tense by the progression of these profits, but linked to the latter usurpation at least partially of intermediaries who undertook to intervene in this process. The livings, the feudal serfdom have changed in appearance, but without changing the essence: alienation due to labour has not disappeared for the population of workers.

Understand how "it works" how to operate such tools guess about what propels originally system cyclic production-consumption, in this case the labour force. Always in effect, create enough to satisfy the two existential needs of man on Earth: his **food** and **protection**, in all senses of the terms, in any material form or not. **Communication**, a system of symbols (language and figures) that he used for these purposes, and it uses more and more to provide indispensable liaisons to the satisfaction of its needs. This is to inform on the values that are attached and how to exchange them, i.e. with the currency. You deduct that the economy is an information system, generic term that applies to any process to get a product, material or not, in order to know the value, then modify it and pass it.

The human economy

Economy of a company or of a country cannot be summed up in this one alliance, numbers encryption and language of the value of production. All these systemic actions certainly calls production, but they would give one an incomplete vision of the economy from the only interpretation of its encryption. Dealing with the past, it does not fully explain the present, can let alone predict the future, since we must stop any process in advance to be able to examine the results (see box). But what characterizes the economic life is precisely the movement of labour. The study of the economy in this book will be therefore built both on the *information*, the values that make it work, on its dynamic of exchanges, and the fact that it is the man who anime it. He uses this money which, curiously, as you will see in detail, is not the reality, - this is the problem - but a mathematical abstraction that it represents. The investigation will be to directly query the sources of systems, to know the objectives which have determined their creation. Inverse method for the traditional economists who analyze the first results to understand the decisions that have been taken to the origin to achieve these results. Here is the choice of inductive system of investigation against the deductive one. That allows us to avoid numbers for its mathematic solutions.

Either those who directly affect the economy, by their purchases, or leaders responsible for the management of their country who receive money from the same individuals, their choices are not neutral. They guide the economy as a result of decisions, whose validity cannot be guaranteed. What may still allow some predictions, but only in the very short term (see box). The whole of society, trained of individuals consumers, is still handled. They are dependent on their needs. By using the method that has computer course - follow the path of the data and results from forces that propel them - it is possible to propose several economic models that should enable policymakers to choose what they think is the best to achieve the results expected. The difficulty is whether it is in favor of human progress, and to what extent. There will always be uncertainties about the evolution of the process in the medium and long term for the overall development, due to contingencies, external circumstances that may influence the course. These processes are system. Therefore, from this perspective, the possible control of the economic system that carries this essay.

This is an essay about money, and how it functions in an advanced industrial economy: i.e. The French economy taken as an exemplary case study. As it happens, it has not been written by a quantitatively-orientated economist, as is often the case, nor a physicist in any strict disciplinary sense of the term. Nevertheless, many of the phenomena that we will be studying will find their direct template in the physical sciences. More specifically, the economy will be seen as a mechanical system drawing its strength from the force animating human agency, this force in turn deriving from that of nature. In this way, the basic existential needs of man are secured: food, protection, shelter, as well as the networks of comunication which secure these primary needs. And beyond these, of course, lie the infinite spiritual needs of man. In this light, it will thus be necessary to consider the economy in its more intangible aspects, and, in particular, take into account the way in which it often singularly fails to cater for the spiritual needs of man. The direct consequence of this deficiency, of course, is that it needs to furnish an ever-greater number of goods and services which purport to meet these needs.

Modern economies thus develop in relation to these primary impulses. Moreover, these impulses, often deeply transient and psychological in aspect, remain elusive when read exclusively through econometric indicators. How, then, can we begin to understand the development of a modern economy in such a way that we might begin to guide it in a more progressive direction? Is such an understanding possible in the face of the pervasive complexity of the whole modern economic system? In the face of such complexity, this essay will propose a very specific analytical model as a way of gaining some kind of purchase on these complex and elusive phenomena: it will be looking at the modern economy as an interdependent network of information systems[1].

The will imparted to these information systems is multiply-forged as is depends upon the interest of *four different actors* (see figure-1): (i) the *population* as a whole; (ii) *private companies*; (iii) *financial institutions*; and (iv) *the State*. It is precisely through these groups that money circulates, and through this process of circulation that human activity assumes monetary value. Moreover, each of these groups also exerts its own specific pressure upon human affairs, acting

---

1 **Information,** to give each thing its due name, confers life upon it. The philosopher, Henri Bergson, gave the name of *élan vital* to the manifold activities of Man on Earth. Since the formation of the Universe, each element which has reached our planet, each elementary particle, constitutes a piece of energized information developing and evolving within a network of interconnected systems, albeit autonomously (see Darwin's theory of determinism). Man, for his part, intervenes in his own environmental system in a more or less constant way, in the hope of modifying this information system to his own advantage.

specifically in its own interest. The actions of the State are also prompted by self-interest; as the institution which controls the money supply, it can expand or contract the latter at will, imparting to it a greater or lesser economic force within the overall system of circulation. This specific dynamic system has, of course, received its particular historical moniker in the post-war period: **monetarism**.

This macroeconomic study will thus be using an original methodology based predominantly upon information-systems technology in order to analyse the modern economy viewed as a dynamic network of information systems automatically transforming raw materials into primary products, primary products into new ones[2].   These systems of production are animated by the primary existential needs that we noted above: food, shelter, communication. Moreover, it is not just material products which enter into circulation within these information systems, but also spiritual ones: everyday pleasures, well-being, communal services, art and culture, all of which have become increasingly deeply inscribed within the cash nexus; all adding their contribution to the Gross National Product. Obviously, it would be somewhat gratuitous to reduce the value of a modern economy to a simple set of figures, as one would be tempted to do for a private company. Nor, as the renowned 18th century economist, Adam Smith, noted, can the

---

2   Second principle of thermodynamics.

modern economy be managed like a family budget. This is primarily a result of the paradoxical rôle of the money system, which, even at the very root of the system of exchange, has a tendency to distort the value of the goods which enter into this system. It is in the light of such distortion that I am going to endeavour to explain how this system has functioned from the inception of our quantitative understanding of it; the novelty in my approach, however, will be that I will not be resorting to quantification; a considerable boon, perhaps, for those of my fellow citizens who might balk at the very sound of the word *economics.*

Indeed, it will be this relational perspective which will enable me, as an information-systems specialist, to link up within one coherent model the different monetary movements issuing from the four principal actors that we have identified. We will also be studying the interrelationship between these different systems of movement. Looking to the pragmatic utilization of our analytical model, it is to be hoped that conclusions may be drawn from it in governmental circles with respect to how society as a whole might be improved, or, at least, certain social classes might benefit. Both governors and the governed might thus become more aware of the systemic parameters governing their own sphere of operation.

This complex articulation which links money to the vital systems of activity and production in modern society was, of course, brilliantly elucidated by J.M. Keynes in his now canonical *General Theory of Employment, Interest and Money* (1936). In this seminal work, Keynes focussed principally on these three aspects of the functioning of the macro-economy to the exclusion of all others, using a mathematical logic which translated a motile physical world. This focus will also inform the study which is to follow; however, it will be integrated within our polysystemic perspective, with special emphasis being placed upon the rôle of the State. Accordingly, all elements at stake within a given system will be construed as units of information which furnish a global view of its mechanisms, by showing the way in which objectives are fulfilled.

It is, ultimately, to be hoped that, by revisiting monetarism in this way, rather in the same way that Keynes implicitly did, we might open up a window of enlightenment for the uninitiated in a world where quantitative methods of understanding do not always take into account polysystemic patterns of exchange and movement.

Within the general system of monetary circulation, featuring four sub-systems controlled by four actors, each acting within its respective rôle, each having benefited from the manna conferred upon it by money; this money is in turn withdrawn by three of the four actors (represented within nodes F2, F3 and B). Having thus withdrawn this liquidity, they then re-inject part of it back into the system in such a way as to boost it, through a kind of leverage mechanism generated by this withdrawal.

This impulse in turn causes the rotational speed of monetary circulation to increase. In this way, all four actors benefit financially from the circulating liquidity, the compound effect of which is that the economy itself grows. This occurs principally after the cyclical withdrawal and is concomitant upon the re-injection of new liquidity into the system, the latter representing added value which factors into overall growth.

This diagram (Fig. 1) gives an integrated representation of various movements in monetary volume in circulation. It enables us to determine how, at each passage through a given mode of exchange, ,it is possible to either introduce or put a brake on liquidity flow with a view to either boosting or dampening consumption.

The introduction of the two national currencies enable us to make an analytical distinctions between, on the one hand, the movement of funds initiated with a purely speculative intention, and, on the other, those initiated in order to facilitate commercial exchange, following the inscription of the surplus value of private enterprise in a different currency.

This diagram gives an integrated representation of the various movements in monetary volume in circulation. It enables us to determine how, at each passage through a given mode of exchange, it is possible to either introduce or put a brake on liquidity flow with a view to either boosting or dampening consumption.

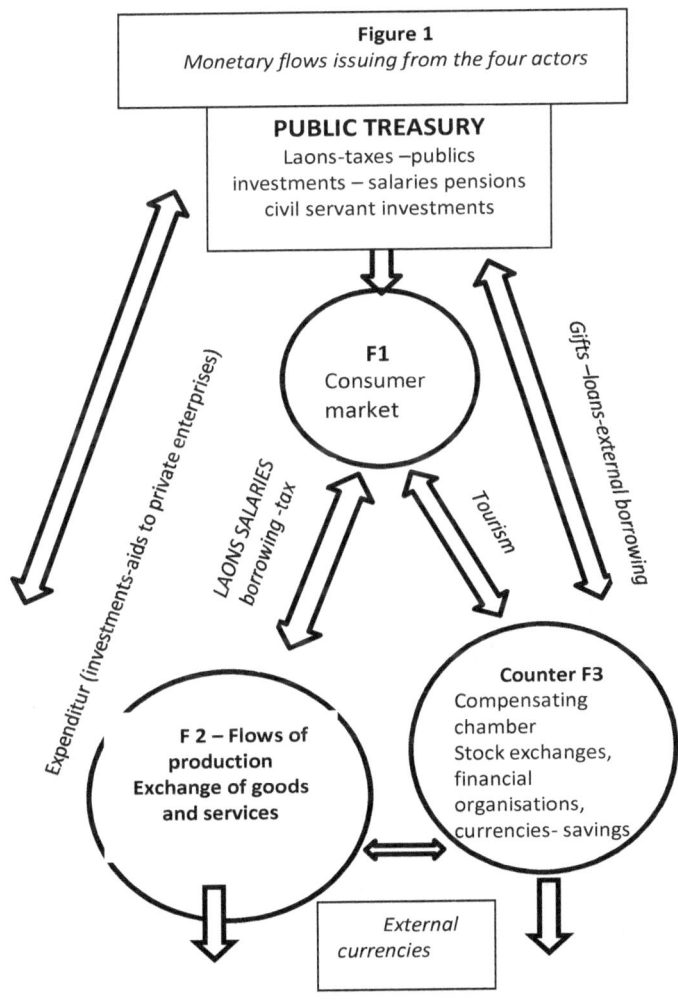

Figure 1
Monetary flows issuing from the four actors

PUBLIC TREASURY
Laons-taxes –publics
investments – salaries pensions
civil servant investments

F1
Consumer
market

Expenditur (investments-aids to private enterprises)

LAONS SALARIES
borrowing -tax

Tourism

Gifts –loans-external borrowing

F 2 – Flows of production
Exchange of goods and services

Counter F3
Compensating
chamber
Stock exchanges,
financial
organisations,
currencies- savings

External currencies

F1: This constitutes the exchange market for all manufactured products (i.e. purchases by the general population), whether these are eventually consumed or not. This category includes all durable or semi-durable products. Moreover, it is this group which forms the basis of all economic activity, and thus of the Economy in general. Everything thus enters into the market mechanism and then passes out of it again. Indeed, it is the general population, in receipt of various revenues, which remains in possession of that portion of liquidity which is in active circulation (at the present moment in France, this represents approximately 60% of the total volume of liquidity in circulation)[3]. Nevertheless, although this group remains the principal agent in the process, it does not actually exert any active influence upon monetary flows. It simply receives monetary remuneration in relation to its value as transformed labour, thus incentivizing producers to reproduce this value. Functioning as a simple relayer of initiatives taken above and beyond its immediate scope of influence, the working population remains effectively passive within the system.

F2: The company invests in production and distribution in the markets for merchandise and

---

3   A few decades ago, it was 70%. NB. Each increase in the money supply can lead directly to inflation by way of compensation for the loss in the unitary value of the currency that such an increase entails.

services. It is then able to generate a financial yield boosted by the surplus value accruing from the labour of its employees. Effectively, it operates as an information-processing centre introducing forces or impulses into monetary circulation which serve to speed it up when positive; or, conversely, to slow it down when negative (see following chapter). In the first case, it is productive investment which serves as a lever in as much as it accelerates the speed of monetary circulation. Effectively, it rewards the **risk-taking aspect presupposed by every financial transaction.** Principally, it is the value generated by labour which serves as the basis for this acceleration. This only occurs, of course, in the case of positive results (surplus value). The importance of this process is two-fold within a free-enterprise context as one portion of the financial results is distributed in the form of salary to the workers and the other within the company itself (self-financing) as well as to providers of external capital in certain cases. Indeed, we have seen one of our recent French Presidents propose that the money accruing to the private company should in turn be distributed in three equal parts: a third in salary; a third distributed to shareholders; and a third to the State in the form of taxes. It goes without saying that this putative division of wealth is completely arbitrary, principally because it does not take into account the freedom of the private company to distribute accrued gains as it sees fit within the private enterpise system.

F3: injected into the system by independent financial institutions in the form of loans, or purchases, the impulse given by the injection of new liquidity into monetary circulation is directly linked to speculative interest[4] accruing from individuals, from private companies, and from the State. In this respect, the notion of interest comes to acquire its full meaning. Here, the impulse is not linked to value accruing from labour but rather from resources generated from within the world of finance itself. Financial interest in turn accrues from this process of internal generation, with a leverage effect operated by the injection of surplus value. Whether one decries this rôle or not, its range of effects is nevertheless undeniable.

B: injected into the system by the State, whose own interest is not speculative given that its principal motive for action is to furnish services to the population. However, in the case of insufficient money coming into the State coffers, the balance of payments will become negative. In the case of France, the constitutionally-imposed norm is to balance the budget as closely as is feasible at any one time; to this end, the State either borrows or prints money in order to fill in the 'hole'. As the habitual master of such monetary creation, it can inject any amount necessary in order to boost the

---

4 **Speculation** here is used in its primary sense of seeking future advantages and gains. As we shall see later, it is only predatory when undertaken excessively.

speed of monetary circulation, or, alternatively, to compensate for its eventual slow-down. Its responsibility in such a case is total. Moreover, this particular effect is worth underlining as it does not actually take into consideration the origin of money itself. Budgetary income, taxes and levies, and such like, only come into the equation as a complement to this process, coming into play in order to

moderate the importance of expenditure, each individual withdrawal from the system through taxation entailing a certain degree of redundancy in the light of its eventual re-injection into the system of monetary circulation again. Technically, the maintenance of such a deficit is natural; serving the population is a costly business. Furthermore, this policy of taking from one party in order to redistribute to another has only one discernible interest (taking this word in the fullest of senses): i.e. targeted redistribution of wealth. In any case, this money is sometimes re-invested (in order to generate a budgetary multiplier effect), the State itself fulfilling the rôle of producer or investor (lender). Indeed, it is precisely for this reason that Keynes has always advocated the prioritizing of State expenditure, especially during a period of deceleration, even if this means incurring larger budget deficits. All this can occur, of course, in tandem with the ongoing boosting of general economic activity through the remuneration of workers within the public sector.

Our governors are thus the principal agents within the process of economic development because it is they who hold the responsibility for producing and distributing this money throughout the population, all of which forms the very basis of the system of monetary circulation.

Principally, it is always the worker who, by dint of his purchases in the general retail market, maintains the process of monetary circulation. Moreover, it is precisely the fulfilment of the worker's needs which stimulates the demand for manufactured goods. This in turn augments the value of the wealth accruing after exchange in the market of material and other goods, this whole process being sustained and transmitted by the money supply. Furthermore, it is from this imperative that the need to maintain a given velocity in the circulation of money arises, thus facilitating the redistribution of wealth as a result of ongoing liquidity injections from the other agents, albeit in certain cases only to offset potential dips in financial performance on the part of each individual agent.

All of the agents mentioned above can have a very tangible impact upon the way in which the national economy develops. Moreover, the State, in its rôle as the most redistributive agent, normally has the necessary means at its disposal to correct any undesirable fluctuations in the money supply induced by budgetary measures. And, subject to prevailing regulations, it can also determine interest rates and thus control financial fluctuations.

In summary, we can see that responsibility for the functioning of the system of monetary circulation, as it pertains to the economy is general, is clearly established among several different actors. In the light of this division of responsibility, we will now proceed to examine in further detail each of the different systems pertaining to the respective actors. In particular, the question needs to be asked: what do they actually do with the money which passes through their hands (a process which I have labelled 'reprocessing' [*retraitment*])? In order to understand this, it will be necessary to deepen our acquaintance with the tool used by each and every one of the agents mentioned above: money.

BOX-1:
SYSTEMS OF THE LIFE FORCE (Bergson's *élan vital*).

Entropy: the 1st principle of thermodynamics

The explosive expansion giving rise to the formation of the universe propels the resulting forces in multiple directions. As a result, the elementary particles bearing this force (vectors), exploding in a random way, then combine and diversify. These diverse combinations and separations gave rise to the formations of the universe that we know today.

The 2nd principle of thermodynamics
Information processing in living systems

These forces, by extending their range of movements, acted to create life on our planet. From system to system, from stage to stage, Man 'burns up' calories (just as all living creatures do) by exploiting these forces in motion in a space-time articulation configured to the scale of our world. Each stage progressively follows the transformation of the state of a given good into another one. The alleviation of the suffering and the forces bearing down upon Man during his labor is nothing less than a vital necessity. This generally comes about through the production of material and immaterial goods. Recently, this production process has been structured by the operations of the monetary system. These vectorized forces generated by the exchange between Man and Nature effectively constitute units of information which will henceforth be traced, inventoried and analyzed in the dynamic form of monetarism.

The paradoxical role of money

Money is a form of monetary circulation which enjoys quasi-stability. Functioning as a means of comparison, it enables the **attribution of specific value to goods and services.** Moreover, the economic school of monetarism highlights the particular rôle played by money, which has only become important in the last few hundred years or so, a negligible period in anthropological terms: i.e. The rôle of money in motion. This latter rôle is effectively part of a system which logically should tend toward its own future destruction as a result of the kind of internal contradiction entailed by the functioning of the system itself, a process which is often encountered in the physical sciences. This often intervenes in the form of a side-effect, or some kind of functional deviation, brought about following the transformation of one state into another (constituted by a modification in the spatio-temporal continuum). There is a critical loss of energy, or entropy, which will eventually end up halting the whole process altogether, external intervention notwithstanding[1].

Values in motion take on unknown directions according to the way in which the money that transits these values is used. A characteristic feature of such deviance within a given system is that it only appears at the beginning of the system's functioning. I will thus limit myself to giving certain general indications regarding this preliminary dysfunctioning, particularly in the light of the fact that the motive-springs of human behaviour are often profoundly irrational; more often than not, these initial impulses lead to wholly unforeseen consequences. Indeed, it is precisely for this reason that it is always difficult to predict the efficiency of a given economic action before putting it through empirical controls. Accordingly, the economic system remains indecipherable, if only as a consequence of this difficulty.

A tool only does what it is designed to do. However, it can easily encounter obstacles as soon as it is set to use. Systems will thus develop in accordance with the initial pressure applied; however, their trajectory might then be modified, with greater or lesser speed, and the hoped-for results radically changed. In such a case, the human force thereby engaged needs to be submitted to a corrective agency, often realised through co-operation in the social and political environment in which it develops, in order that the initial intended effects may in fact be realised.

Money used as an instrument of measurement

In the beginning, Man laboured in order to produce the wherewithal to feed himself. He obtained these products by transforming raw materials from the earth, thanks to solar energy: his own labour power, sustained by the food thereby produced, in turn constantly generated further food supplies. Moreover, once he had become sedentary, he invented tools in order to improve the efficiency of his labour, both quantitatively and qualitatively. It was at this point that he began to generate surplus production, which could in turn be exchanged for the surplus production generated by neighbouring producers: man thus emerged as both producer and consumer, as is the case within the tribal unit. At first, this kind of exchange of surplus production occurred in the form of bartering; in this form, the exchange is immediate: open and direct, labour-value exchanged for labour-value, more or less justly evaluated, as in the exchange of gifts.

In the beginning he was the land-owner exploiting with his peers the fruits of the earth. This constituted his wealth, obtained or preserved if need be **by force**. Indeed, the very same principle remains applicable today given that contemporary producers, without relinquishing force, have expanded the surface area of their land, which thence becomes productive land. This expansion necessarily occurs at the expense of the weaker elements of society, comprising the basic workforce which exploits but does not own the land. Accordingly, demographic expansion has brought in its wake a corresponding increase in the number of productive land-owners.

Suspect Money

About 2800 years ago a tool-system in the form of coins was invented, metal money, in order that Man might exchange his own surplus production more easily for other products, in remoter markets, by attributing a conventional value to the goods exchanged; one which had been determined quantitatively in advance. This system was accordingly more precise than barter. The money used as a tool of control and evaluation in relation to these exchanged goods flowed from the private individual into the collectivity and vice versa. Operating as a tool of comparison, acting almost like a set of scales, money had no stable value despite the fact that it had initially been linked to the notion of weight. This objective symbol, conventionally established on a wider scale on the basis of a unitary figure pertinent for all currency, was projected and imposed as a standard measure by the government or authority presiding over the territory concerned. This information was then orientated toward the private individual[12]. In this way money became inscribed as a concrete system of evaluation, neatly labelled, and pertaining to the hidden value of the product entering into its nexus; this value being determined by the producer in accordance with criteria that remained peculiar to him.

The evaluation of such goods also depends upon subjective criteria on the part of the buyer; these are likely to reflect his own wealth and spending power. Indeed, each private consumer is likely to consider a given item as being implicitly more or less expensive in relation to these criteria. In essence, each act of evaluation on the part of the private consumer will be carried out in relation to the yardstick furnished by previous evaluations made of previous acquisitions of a similar nature, recorded in memory with a greater or lesser degree of efficiency and thus more or less approximate in nature. Indeed, although the actual weight of the money thrown upon the scales might be considered to confer upon it some kind of stable measure, there is no real guarantee that the sum total of this mass would correspond to that determined by a separate act of weighing on the part of the producer.

BOX-2 – The experimental laws of systems.

Secondary effects

Corrosion – each movement *systematically* undergoes a partial loss of force due to the cooling-down which occurred following the 'Big Bang'. Any action which is destined to attain a state differing from its initial one does not as a result of caloric force transmit the totality of its own value (the law of Sadi Carnot). It is by taking this side-effect (a residue of the primary force) into account that we will construct the analysis of our own economic system. Indeed, it is in this way that all living systems exhaust themselves such that they require constant replenishment. The 'waste' (or unexploited caloric residues) can be re-used (through re-cycling) within the various sub-systems. It nevertheless becomes inevitable that new waste will be generated in the process. Accordingly, the gains in time and space designed to extend the efficiency of the initial system will become less and less significant, exercising progressively less impact in the process.

Leverage effect

Any given tool, by increasing the initial force exerted,

---

represents a linear lever provided that only the composition of its own matter constitutes the origin of this force: for example, iron is a better tool than bronze or wood for displacing a heavy object. Furthermore, this power will be multiplied if the movement is rotatory; there will also be economies in terms of the time and space required, thus generating a more favorable effect as a result of the more rapid return of the force applied. Indeed, the invention of the wheel stemmed from the application of these very principles.

Changes

Only an **exterior** fulcrum enables a given force to be transmitted (see Box- , p. 16). Indeed, the tracking of a given movement only becomes possible on the basis of an initial or final state. By definition, a movement never ceases during its own course. **Indeed, it is precisely for this reason that one cannot change a system from within if nothing has been designed in advance to meet this end.** Models deduced from systems allow for certain controls and rectifications at the end of the day, but only after the halting of the process itself.

Obstacles – during the transition, the system might encounter unforeseen obstacles issuing from factors pertaining to the world outside.   These obstacles provoke certain dysfunctional disturbances in the system; these can, however, be overcome. Nevertheless, the system, like any tool, remains effectively neutral within this whole process. Any revision thus needs to be carried out *a posteriori*. Accordingly, the ONLY kind of self-regulation possible is that which has been programmed in advance: **one cannot modify a system from within because one simply does not see it.**

All of these considerations do not in any way take into account the modifications carried out by intermediaries who, within the production chain, in turn establish their own price in accordance with criteria established by their own activity. Principal among these criteria are the quality and the rarity of the product concerned; all of which opens the door to various disparities and abuses in different markets, each one of which uses their own set of scales, these scales representing a symbolic tool of measurement pertaining to both the individual and the collectivity, and yet freely acknowledged by both parties as the sole and exclusive tool of exchange. Nevertheless, one might well ask: where are the administrators of these goods, the auctioneers, as it were, the referees who would apply this tool in order to attribute an exact value to a given item which might be universally accepted by all? At the end of the day, money remains an unreliable tool of comparison; although it can be used to attribute a particular value to a given item, it has no intrinsic value in itself. This attribution might thus be judged of suspect validity.

Like any instrument of measurement, it functions by changing an elementary memorized unit into a symbol in order to obtain other values of an equally symbolic order, albeit **displaced**, as occurred with the abacus, which was the first instrument used in primitive societies to confer a different signification upon material values. In this way, quantity accruing through the accumulation of different figures (symbols) becomes inscribed within space. This operation, involving as it does the displacement of one value into another, is nothing more or less than a form of word processing. The abacus used in this way as a means of evaluating a given item, a function which is in no way gratuitous, thus becomes the fundamental formula governing the act of labour : labour = force applied over time and in space resulting in the production of a given item. This calculation is a way of determining these quantities, offering variable results in relation to the desired objective; more or less work carried out generating a greater or lesser degree of value according to the case. The same considerations hold for writing, the latter displacing a referent into symbolic space: the letter, completed within the unity of the word, and then within that of the sentence, and thereafter recursively within the body of the text, finally acquiring a sense[3] within the systemic logic of the latter. The same system of symbolic value obtains in the economic sphere, words and numbers being used to evaluate human activity, processed in such a way that these units of information acquire signification only after being displaced.

We have seen that the system of scales was not able to confer any certainty upon these comparative results at the end of the day. The symbol represented by money is only an approximation, which goes some way to explaining the kinds of distortion which it generates. Particularly as one cannot consider this first measure as stable, nor those which ensued in the markets. Indeed, how can one reasonably admit the possibility of a variation of variation? How might this constant volatility be controlled? The money-system, sensitive to outside movements, cannot avoid generating accidents along the way as it evolves and develops. Moreover, monetary-exchange flows serve to accentuate the distortions incurred within exchange values by virtue of their movement alone.

The process of evaluating a given item through money, on the one hand, and ensuring its transmission, on the other, by virtue of the same tool serves to create two different systems which, according to the rôle that one attributes to them, can generate interferences, complicating them to the extent that their reciprocal functions are rendered incoherent. Effectively, the evaluation of any given item which seems to follow the laws of supply and demand has a certain subjective element to it, whereas the transactional process is orientated in terms of destination, conceived of as a simple means of impersonal transport.

It is precisely for this reason that one has to put the traditional law of supply and demand to one side, which, operating in accordance with the presumpton of freedom of evaluation, is supposed to be equitable. Moreover, laws are executed in

order to regulate excesses and errors, in order to countervail the 'dictatorship' of the law of supply and demand, of money circulating within markets.

One can perhaps summarize the workings of this paradoxical system in the following way: on the one hand, one transmits a given item measured in terms of value by the weight of a metal, 'one' buys another item elsewhere which is supposedly possessed of an identical value, measured in the same way by weights recognized as equivalent; however, what is not transmitted is the set of scales that has weighed out these values. The assignment of monetary value providing both instrinsic and extrinsic measurement thus generates results which are, at one and the same time, both true and false. And from this bivalence emerges the paradox that no single guarantee can correct.

Within the monetary system which translates human activity and establishes a system of exchange within diverse kinds of markets, Man is capable of changing roles within this system, becoming either producer and consumer in accordance with his rôle in society. As within the feudal system, he determines given levels of production and purchasing on the basis of a system which is fundamentally flawed.

It will thus always be somewhat fallacious to deduce the real economic value of a given piece of productive activity from the mere calculation of its quantified value, given that the instrument which manipulates these symbols is itself flawed. As a consequence, the assessments offered by the majority of orthodox economists are themselves to be treated with caution as nothing can be adduced to prove that the figures which they are using are accurate in any given case, nor indeed the words which they are using to interpret these figures. A human economy quantified on the basis of the money-system is thus only capable of generating suspect results; all the more so given that another distorting factor intervenes within the system operating as an instrument of exchange.

Let us return to the first method employed by Man to exchange goods: that of barter. In this system, the attribution of value took place in relation to the amount of work necessary for the production of both sets of goods, these being set up in direct confrontation with one another in the here and now. These exchanges were carried out between two parties that were directly present to one another: one single buyer and one single producer. As a result, the scope of these exchanges, although entirely suited to the two parties concerned, could never expand. However, thanks to the advent of money (which we will call B), exchanges could then take place between people who were not physically present to one another. The handicap of distance was thus eradicated. Accordingly, if A and C are items possessed in principle of the same value, and have been evaluated as equal by the arbitrage of B employed as a measuring instrument, equal value can then be attributed to them both with confidence, despite the anonymous nature of the whole transaction.

Nevertheless, this exchange remains suspect for another reason: the theory of systems postulates that the result of a given transfer will change the initial value of a product in the time that it takes to complete the action. There is in effect a time of transit between A and C which corresponds to the transport carried out by B, this deferral in turn serving to skew the original values. A certain period of latency is thus added to each monetary evaluation, accruing as a result of B which serves as a vehicle for this passage between one and the other state. Accordingly, the intermediary value B attributed to given items through equational transposition does not in reality respect the integral value of these measured items. This is not only due to the difficulties entailed by the act of evaluation that we have just seen, but also due to the inconstancy of the value in the transfer. Indeed, this parameter, which seemed to have been ensured by the existence of coins, was at the end of the day only guaranteed by their physical weight. However, in the living realm, and in the physical world upon which this depends, there cannot be any degree of exactitude; the present moment only exists in the abstract *ergo* the time calculated in relation to the reality of a particular movement can only be calculated relatively, but not in absolute terms. Accordingly, calculation in these conditions remains necessarily approximate. If the system of evaluation only involves a very short period of development, the time lost in the transformation induced by the monetary transit from the original item to its goal remains negligible. Nevertheless, the system is capable of transporting highly significant values in relation to monetary volume in the long term; in this case, the results are, accordingly, likely to become more significantly skewed. In addition to this initial distortion, we might also take into account that contributed by the time taken to physically transport the item itself. That said, the latter is, in the final analysis, determinable given that it is visibly factored into the calculation of value by the producer himself.

Everyone knows that money loses its value over time (time is money!). Indeed, any good company manager knows that the volume of current stock should be limited as much as possible because the money that it represents will lose its value over time. Moreover, this erosion of monetary value, a natural side effect of the system itself, has been repeatedly confirmed by historical statistics[4]. Ultimately, we can deduce from this that the money which makes each value imperceptibly but surely drop is nothing more or less than a form of deception.

The law of systems serves to elucidate both a tangible advantage (in this case, that of economic development by the markets) and a pervasive drawback (i.e. the loss of value, a side effect generated by the item in transit operating in accordance with the law of systems).

This loss of residual value is not uniquely incumbent upon the owners of given items that might ultimately be dispensed with, but also upon anyone who might possess liquid assets over a given period of time.

Money, functioning as an instrument of transport, thus adds a negative parameter, diminishing the overall value of the surplus values accruing from production: *eo ipso* this results in the loss of its own value. This underground evaluation, operating independently of the initial value of the transported goods, induces a loss which is entirely intrinsic to the monetary system itself. Moreover, this loss occurs from the moment the currency has been freshly minted, albeit less than tangibly as a result of the slowness of the process of exchange.

Following each act of purchase, given that the purchased items have been poorly evaluated, owner-producers, financiers, the possessors of monetary power, in addition to that of the State, will overestimate the value of given items by way of compensation in order to re-establish a certain general equilibrium, the latter having been slightly diminished by this monetary circulation. These compensations are, moreover, sufficiently light to be practically invisible if the rotational speed of this circulation is low. Although minimal in the case of each transaction, these compensations are multiplied by the enormous quantity exponentially accruing from the sum total of transactions which occur at every minute within all of the markets involving the exchange of value in each country. Of course, the masters of pricing will often pre-empt such losses through nominal rises instigated beforehand; in other words, by extracting more surplus value at a rate which should, at the very least, correspond to the value of the rate of interest prevailing in the credit markets. The latter, dictated by financial institutions, will thus participate in the operation of a perpetual adjustment mechanism compensating for the endemic loss in the value of money induced by the passage of time.

In the beginning, the existence of money enabled Man to respond to the need to extricate himself from the straitjacket of the bartering system, which only permitted the exchange of two items in the here and now. Indeed, no-one would be likely to feel themselves badly done to in transactions of such nature as long as they remained local in scope, entailing only degrees of variation which were barely perceptible. However, the emerging possibility of transmitting items in progressively less constrained environments, within a progressively wider scope of operation, meant, as we have seen, that initial values could only be maintained in an increasingly problematic way, as a function of the multiple compounding of indirect exchanges. The problem with all this, unfortunately, was that this system of quantification, although conventional, and thus guaranteed by obligation through the offices of a public institution, remained potentially nefarious; its usage[5], although serving to liberate the forces of production, also remained at the exclusive disposition of those who owned the land, the site of productive labour; moreover, this land was essentially transmitted through inheritance, as in feudal times, as well as generally having been initially acquired by force. In this way, the exploitative system of surplus extraction imposed by the feudal lords upon the peasants was effectively extended and refined, this time in a form mediated through monetary exchange. Thus, as we can clearly see, the exploitation of the peasant and the worker for the benefit of the boss has an eminently historical origin; this process of exploitation having been inscribed within the system inaugurated by money.

[1]This is the second law of thermodynamics. This kind of autordestruction has also been highlighted by the ecologists, a movement prefigured from the

beginning of the 20th century by certain evolutionist economists such as Georgescu-Roegen

2This point will be highlighted in figure-3 to follow..

3This word is remarkable because it also confers sense upon the process of evolution, ever since the 'Big Bang', issuing from heat and orientating itself toward the cold (entropy).

4See INSEE.

5The value of usage identified by Marx.

i2/ This point will be highlighted in figure-3 to follow.

THE MARKETS: the birth of capitalisms.

The power of the development of the productive market; leverage effects.

From the very moment of its inception, the *élan vital* has given Man the impulse to progress, in the interests of his work, for better or worse. This represents nothing more or less than the particular determinism governing his nature, dictated, as we have seen, as much by his spirituality as his survival instinct. More and more births, and more and more «wealth», in order to at least satisfy these new needs: this is the very law governing the genre of humanity.

Nevertheless, spurred on by the different **interests** animating the actors of the Economy, Man goes way beyond the simple levels of production value which are needed to guarantee his survival by constantly re-injecting supplements of supplements of value into the original system of production; all of which in turn gives him a supplement of productive power. By using the leverage effect afforded by the tool of money, he was thus able to expand the scope of these basic exchanges into fully-fledged markets. Moreover, ultimately, this primary phenomenon can be appealed to in order to explain the existence of large multinational companies generated by long-term increases in productive power operating in tandem with the acquisition of progressively greater market share.

From this, we can see that money has acquired an autonomous power by virtue of the sole fact of its circulation; this power, enhanced by the phenomenon of monetary self-generation, enables

a constant increase in the volume of goods in circulation, be they material[5] or spiritual.

In order to be efficient, any tool requires some kind of force or leverage when it comes to transforming a particular product issuing from one state into another. Moreover, this transformation will be achieved with an increase in value in relation to the original product, more often than not accruing due to gains made in time as well as sometimes in space. Indeed, this was precisely the way things occurred with the plough, which used the force of both the ox and the ploughshare as tools in order to increase the yield of corn harvested through expansion of the total land mass sown[6]. In this way, gains in both time and space accrued in relation to the work that a single man equipped with a spade would have needed to carry out. Moreover, in order to ensure its basic maintenance, each and every system requires a constant increase in the force animating it to occur. Each unit of force which is

---

5   As long as there are sufficient resources, as well as control of their side effects, i.e.waste products.

6   N.B. The peasant farmer kept back a portion of the grain issuing from his harvest in order to sow afresh. If he kept back a portion greater than his immediate needs, he was thereby able to increase his future harvest provided that he was also able to expand the total surface of arable land available to him. As it happens, this particular system of production is actually forbidden by law: he is now obligated to buy his grain from a multinational. Thus, we find the same leverage effect as occurs through the circulation of money, valid for any producer who reintroduces his surplus value into the production system (thus self-financing).

supplementary in relation to that representing the basic threshold of maintenance serves thus to increase the sum of value produced, becoming in the process wealth to be accumulated. Furthermore, it is the eventual re-utilisation of the marginal value (i.e. surplus value or profit) produced which serves to either constantly maintain or to increase the level of production thereby established. In the light of all this, we can see that there is nothing particularly mysterious about the impulsion given by money – the contingent bearer of all value – nor indeed its prevailing power, when **it comes be invested** to in the system of production; systemic gains accrue all round from this process. These gains issue from the different ways of processing units of information-force.

Productive capitalism emerges at the same time as the invention of the motor engine. The early 18th century engines were initially steam-powered (Denis Papin), giving rise to the first forms of mass production in the craft workshops, these having hitherto produced piecemeal. Moreover, these workshops were often clustered around the mining regions in order that they might benefit from the proximity of the coal which drove their engines. Their territory was thus necessarily limited. However, by the beginning of the 19th century, these had been supplanted by electrical motors, which were smaller and easier to power, as well as internal combustion engines, which were easier to transport. Both of these innovations enabled the rise of the capitalist system proper brought about by the increase in monetary wealth accruing from the time saved within the process of production. Conversely, the advent of textile machinery also had a big impact on employment as soon as it was introduced, as was seen notably in Lyon, France (1930) in the *révolte des Canut.* In this way, new factories proliferated right across North-America, as well as in the manufacturing hub of Northern Europe, notably, within France, Germany, and Great Britain; indeed, all of these countries were in the process of changing their economies thanks to the newly unleashed energy resources generated by the transformation of coal power into electrical power.

The over-increase in the power of money due to monetary rotation.
We can see in figure-2 that money circulates within an almost closed system – in the opposite direction to that of goods purchased. The buyer receives these goods, but he gives money to the eventual distributor of them, who then retransmits them in stages to the initial producer. This system, which enables the transportation of all kinds of product, material or otherwise, within the monetary system of the markets, is very much a circular affair; this is because it is **the same global sum**, the monetary volume, which constantly serves to facilitate the exchange of goods, and thus to support production. Accordingly, the purchased item in turn induces a further solicitation at the level of demand,

which is (at least partially) always satisfied by the purchase of products.[7] Moreover, in global terms, this circular system of forces propelled by the configuration of buyer-sellers remains, as we have seen, bound by the law dictating the wearing down of all systems as a result of their variously articulated motions. In this way, it becomes caught within a vicious circle, whose downward spiral it recurrently traces, at the same time constantly increasing itself due to the effect of supplementary forces introduced by way of compensation. These forces animate the system with each transit, thanks to surplus values accruing from various different sources[8], all of which generates a kind of snowball effect at each stage of transformation. The leverage effect generated by each and every tool is thus further dynamized by this movement, particularly given that it is circular[9].

---

7 This is a figure generally known to the central banks, who will set about adjusting variations thereof.

8 This processing of information presupposes that each of the products which transit effectively serve to transport both the origins and the objectives of the system used, these systems having been set in motion by the intervention of actors. Moreover, the deviant effects accumulated in the course of these events might well provoke specific conditions of crisis according to the case.

9 Force of the couple.

BOX-3: The exercise of will in the Economy.

Having become aware of **information** relating to the inefficiency of his work, this information being relayed by his own **senses**, the monkey who has picked up too small a stone to crack open the coconut will modify his tool-system accordingly by picking up a bigger one. Having **physically relayed** the material forces coming under his command from the outside world, he then **reflects mentally** on their use. These two actions, physical and mental respectively, issue from the use of initial caloric forces.

Man, as indeed any animal, becomes aware of the results of his actions by means of experimentation, conducted with the aid of his own senses. He can increase the efficiency of the tool-system by making rectifying adjustments or, if need be, simply choosing a better tool. On the basis of a process of trial and error (which effectively constitutes a series of **reflections**), he can set about overcoming any unforeseen obstacles. He researches and develops (through invention) new tools in the constantly renewed effort to feed himself. He also **reflects** upon the best **methods** of increasing the yield of his labor by using the forces at his disposal. Thanks to the constant invention of new tools, Man has thus for millions of years been able to increase his own capacity for both adaptation and comprehension **through the exercise of his own agency.** He has, similarly, become better equipped to evaluate and distinguish the values (both material and spiritual) that interest him as he forges on in the direction which he has elected to pursue.

Let us remain for a moment in the physical domain. Given that money is possessed of an intrinsic power, the 'centrifugal' force generated by the rotation of purchasing forces in circular movement (as is the case with all phenomena of this kind) will show a tendency to deviate outwards if the equilibrium established between the forces of centripetal and centrifugal pressure, respectively, show themselves to be unequal. Symbolically, the circular partition constituted by the exchange of products can at this point be considered to be effectively porous, a certain portion of the sum total value leaking toward private enterprise, financial institutions, and the State. Thus, the force of the lever-money is multiplied by this centrifugal force, harvested firstly by the producer. It then returns to the latter in order to boost his production, or, at the very least, to maintain it, all of which constitutes a basic kind of more-or-less regular redistribution of the values thereby produced. If, on the other hand, the sum of liquidity generally diminishes, there will not be any kind of equitable redistribution in favour of the actors controlling the circulation of money, each one of these henceforth finding themselves in a position of acute competition determined by their respective interests and attractions. Needless to say, this is only the case within a liberal system.

Furthermore, acceleration might issue from the supply side of the equation, for example, if the information about quality, price and reputation transmitted through advertising has an **incentivizing** effect inducing a greater volume of purchasing (see figure-2). These phenomena might be categorized as psychological effects which enter into the equation as drivers propelling money into its rôle as a primary force. Moreover, we can also appeal to these phenomena when taking into account the will of the various actors who make the decisions which finally lead to a given act of purchase, acts of expenditure. Ultimately, the sum total of these acts will eventually determine whether the circular movement animating the totality of the various exchange markets in operation will be successfully articulated with the system of production or not. At the end of the day, the acceleration , or alternatively the deceleration, of the speed of rotation will depend upon such factors. Furthermore, the exercise of this will presupposes a certain degree of trust regarding the results of the various acts of processing undertaken by each actor operating within their respective domains. Indeed, each act of purchase constitutes, at one and the same time, both an act of acquisition in the present and an investment in the future: i.e. a kind of propulsion toward a result to be realised prospectively. This is by no means anodyne as we can appeal to the compounded consequences of such acts of prospective orientation in order to explain the development and growth of certain companies into multinationals, simply by virtue of the progressive increase in their productive power (the latter in turn being dependent upon consumer confidence). We might summarize this line of influence by saying that the confidence transmitted from the consumer to the producer enables the latter in turn to plan for and invest in new production projects.

Using such data, we might hope to explain the various crises of under- and over-production which have occurred in accordance with the degree of reciprocal confidence afforded to the population of producers on the part of the population of consumers. Furthermore, this kind of confidence can not be prescribed from above; rather, it is inspired on the basis of promising results.This will, of course, depend upon the psychological factors that we have elucidated (above); these factors contributing to the overall level of satisfaction felt by the consumer relative to the quality of the response evoked by their demand. Product price, which obviously varies over time, is thus no longer the only criterion to take into account. Figures-3 and -4 demonstrate how this confidence works through the system by presenting it in terms of a physical articulation. We have, of course, already encountered this word several times in the course of our exposition. It provides a permanent accompaniment to our elucidation of money in its various different guises. Moreover, as a result of this purely psychological value, slippages can occur between the circular and the productive movements in train, thereby provoking the kind of production crises to which I have referred. Thanks to this representation of the productive system, which deals with the various movements issuing from human action, I have been able to show that the Economy is an integrated system articulating both the physical and the psychological aspects of economic activity, conceptualized jointly under the category of information. In particular, one can see how reactions are provoked within the productive system linked to Man through labour (figure-4): it shows that it is monetary circulation which constitutes the basis of employment, a factor which is easily forgotten when one considers that it is the private company from which employment originates. Ultimately, however, the private company must be considered to be a consequence rather than a cause of productive labour, albeit one which has become an indispensable concomitant of the latter.

As regards the totality of production, the activity of a country varies and can slow down at any given time, albeit without ceasing completely; the latter representing a technical impossibility as long as there are still men alive to produce.

In each and every case, to invest is to speculate: i.e. to expect a supplementary return on value by virtue of the leverage effect in operation. There is a permanent risk that the leverage effect operated by money will in fact become inoperative as a result of the absence of accrued surplus value obtaining in the event of ill-usage. Anomalies might also result from the presence of unforeseen obstacles blocking the pathways of the systems in action; all of which might eventually lead to losses.

Even the fact of setting oneself up as a simple craftsman represents an act of speculation to the extent that one wishes to obtain advantages from one's work. Furthermore, any act of purchase can also be considered an act of speculation in that it necessarily entails risks: as long as the purchaser has not taken full possession of the good concerned, he will not be able to appreciate it fully. Even on a small scale, knowing the price of something does not necessarily enable one to ascertain its quality; the degree of satisfaction procured involving a strong degree of subjective evaluation. (see chapter on "Suspect Money").

If this depends upon **the right or wrong use of the money reinvested, the risk will be proportional to the latter's volume in relation to what the purchaser can afford.** Only the kind of **confidence** which guarantees results in conformity with forecasts and experience enables decision-making to be carried out in the least perilous way possible (see Figure-2). Indeed, this wholly psychological aspect involving the exercise of free-will within the workings of the economic system has been clearly brought to the forefront of our understanding by J.M. Keynes. Moreover, this factor also has severe consequences for any understanding of the Economy which is based upon a purely mathematical understanding of the relevant statistics and figures, particularly in the light of the fact that these figures are likely to vary in direct relation to the degree of confidence obtaining among consumers at any given moment in time.

When it is wisely employed, this money-tool can bring in an extra dose of liquidity which can then be spread through each linked system, in a chain reaction which serves to develop economic activity and enables critical thresholds to be breached. This cyclical leverage effect impacting upon monetary circulation, and operating through forces in motion, should be considered in a purely mechanical way.

Production is capable of fructifying and expanding the Economy at every level of operation[10], provided that it allows for a redistribution either in the form of wages in the public sector or in the form of public assistance, and also provided that this redistribution is devoted entirely to expenditure. In this way, the economic development of a country becomes tributary to the driving role of the Welfare State, recent virulent criticism of the latter notwithstanding. On this occasion, too, political decisions are prompted by psychological motives, as indeed are all human decisions.

The Economy is very much the fruit of human activity. The real Economy is constituted by

---

[10] One must nevertheless exclude second-order expenditure within the system: i.e. the intrinsic corrosion of the system of money in circulation, which will in no sense be compensated for by a readjustment in the value of goods thereby represented. This can be seen, for example, in the built-in obsolescence and destruction of military weaponry.

production which has been sold in the consumer market, the latter to be understood in its widest sense: i.e. everything which can be **bought and sold,** everyday household goods, semi-durable or durable goods, etc. Indeed, this money becomes indispensable as it circulates globally.

The purchasing power resulting from labor can only be factored into the equation determining a sound relationship between employment and finance by the State itself: wage earners, despite their role as the principal drivers of the Economy, have no *direct* control over its functioning, being neither producers nor distributors nor financiers. Indeed, it is precisely for this reason that Keynesian economists postulate the need for the State to intervene by controlling, not only its own expenses but also the monetary volume constituted by the expenditure of wage earners and financial institutions[11]. Moreover, it is important to realize that an equitable and efficient redistribution of wealth is only rendered possible if the monetary volume issuing from these sectors can be brought into operational harmony, despite their nominally discrete spheres of operation. At this point in our exposition, it is important to remind ourselves that all economic systems and sub-systems are linked within the general network of monetarism. The

---

[11] The three actors in this system effectively form a three-threaded system, reminiscent of a Gordian knot; impossible to unravel, and thus to arrange harmoniously, when only one thread is tackled.

equitable redistributive functioning of these systems and sub-systems is in turn premised upon the assumption that no one party will divert an excessive portion of liquidity from another in pursuit of its own interest. Ultimately, any act of speculation which rides roughshod over these finely-articulated and inter-dependent links is liable to become a predatory and nefarious one, as much for its agent as those who submit to its consequences.

For example, financial institutions tend to keep a strict eye on interest rates as it is they who furnish the credit which serves to boost the purchasing power of given sectors of the population that might otherwise be deprived of spending opportunities. This is particularly the case in the market for durable and semi-durable goods. This is clearly demonstrated in F-3 in Figure-1. Nevertheless, this credit facility can often result in excessive pressure being exercised by financial institutions as they strive to maximize revenue from interest – this is motivated by nothing more or less than sheer greed, as Joseph Stieglitz has pointed out. And in the wake of such excesses comes the risk of systemic break-up, leading to a dramatic dip in the volume of liquidity circulating within the 'pipework' of liquidity circulation. It is precisely as a result of these dysfunctional tendencies that the need to operate a clear filtering process arises, both internally and externally, conceived with the aim of ironing out excessive accumulation in any one part of the system. In particular, I would wish to advocate the establishment of an internal currency which would be wholly specific to the financial sector, for example, the *Ecu* in France. Through the operation of this device, the State might be able to intervene in given instances by blocking the issuing of liquidity in order to prevent any possible crisis resulting from the inordinate swelling of monetary volume (as was the case in the recent 'sub-prime' crisis).

Despite these vagaries threatening to skew the system, growth remains the source of wealth, which requires above all an equitable distribution in order that productive employment be maintained, notwithstanding the fact that the latter is becoming more and more based upon the production of non-material goods in contemporary advanced economies. In order for the level of employment to be either maintained or increased to its maximum level in these economies (a feat which has proven to be historically possible), a permanently increasing growth rate is required (see figure-3). The three previous actors, each one at their own level generating the required money, the latter having been effectively extorted from the population of consumers by virtue of price rises imposed by distributors and producers, as well as by virtue of the interest owed to the banks, and the increase in liquidity issuing from the printing of money by the State in accordance with its budgetary needs.

Property: the predatory power of capital.

When *homo erectus,* who had effectively evolved into *homo sapiens,* invented tools in order to improve the quality of his daily life, he was both producer and consumer of his own sustenance. As his work evolved and began to produce more than was strictly necessary to meet his subsistence needs, he disposed of the surplus by bartering with his neighbors. Moreover, he remained, along with his peers, the owner of the earth from which he drew this sustenance. This constituted the source of his wealth, obtained and preserved generally by dint of force. The power of money remained in turn relatively stable when the system developed feudal forms; this was principally because it was maintained as such within restricted localities by the most powerful members of the community, village chiefs and other figures invested with seniority and authority.

Essentially, nothing has really changed since, taking into account that productive land has subsequently been divided and distributed through various proprietorial decrees. In our present liberal system the power that had initially been acquired through the violence of possession subsists, in a form regulated by the rights of ownership. In its role as evaluator and transmitter of goods, money also transmits the violence inherent in the very notion of property. This principle still applies today, to the extent that certain parties have been able to increase the land surface in their possession by applying the force of money to the detriment of other parties; these lands then being put to productive use. Moreover, with demographic expansion came the concomitant increase in the numbers of the exploited. All of this, of course, has been widely recognized; nevertheless, it remains important to acknowledge it afresh when reviewing the fundamental principles of macroeconomic theory.

Paraphrasing the French social philosopher, Proudhon, "property is theft"; rephrasing a little, we might express this dictum alternatively in terms of the predatory violence of owners toward the dispossessed, the new serfs.

The secondary effects inherent in each and every system are more or less rapidly compounded until deviant or corrosive (*usure*) consequences ensue; moreover, it is no coincidence that the word usury (referring to the establishment of excessive interest rates for lending) bears the same etymological roots as *usure* (= corrosive wear and tear) in French. All of which serves to put severe brakes on the operation of the monetary system, even to the extent that the latter becomes threatened with extinction, a catastrophic eventuality that will only be warded off provided that the initial force animating the system can be re-boosted with a view to counteracting this entropic effect. The maintenance of the system will be further strengthened if a certain degree of internal regulation can be integrated with a view to counteracting and repelling these toxic side-effects. Moreover, these side effects can perhaps be fruitfully compared to those of a 'hidden vice' as it is rarely at the level of current use that they become manifest. All of which explains the presence of residual structural inflation due to the constant increase in the volumes of money in circulation, on the back of which increases in prices only occur by way of compensation for the effect of corrosion thus entailed.

As in each and every system, the side effects generated by the movements ensuing from the transformation and distribution of profits can throw up obstacles in the wake of these movements. This can be a result of either excesses or insufficiency according to the period; a poor interpretation on the basis of the index created by the number of purchases can lead in turn to a poor appreciation of the number of items to produce. These interpretive distortions then give rise to crises of under- or over-production which can subsequently degenerate into fully-blown financial crises. These crises, needless to say, usually have profoundly negative consequences for the economic development of the countries concerned, particularly if the benefits accruing from any foreign trade are also insufficient to ensure an issue therefrom.

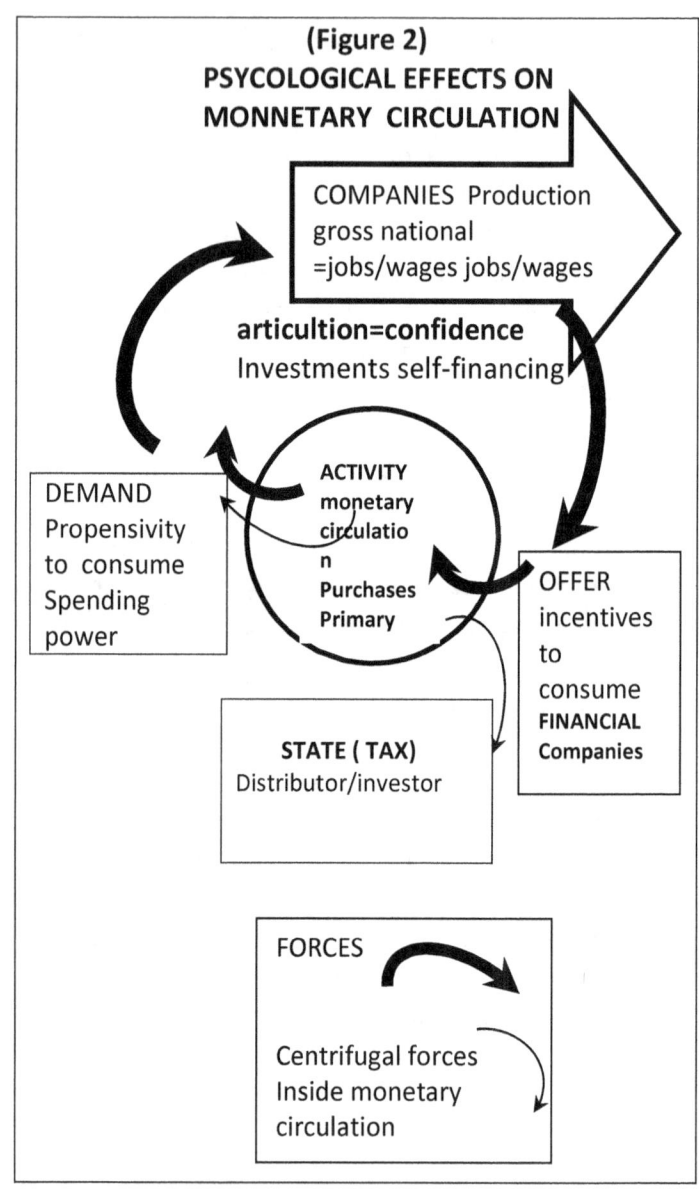

(Figure 2)
**PSYCOLOGICAL EFFECTS ON
MONNETARY CIRCULATION**

COMPANIES Production
gross national
=jobs/wages jobs/wages

articultion=confidence
Investments self-financing

ACTIVITY
monetary
circulatio
n
**Purchases
Primary**

DEMAND
Propensivity
to consume
Spending
power

OFFER
incentives
to
consume
FINANCIAL
Companies

STATE (TAX)
Distributor/investor

FORCES

Centrifugal forces
Inside monetary
circulation

This principally mechanical mode of functioning

due at the outset to the nature of labor power, be it material or intellectual, can be adduced to explain the supplementary increments of surplus value accruing from the rotatory leverage effect. Losses in value can also be explained in this way. The more the speed of monetary circulation either increases or diminishes, the more significant the latter are likely to be. However, this dispersion of wealth – constituted by the units of surplus value which are not returned in totality to the productive system – is usually taken advantage of by those parties who have a vested interest in the system of monetary circulation, which will henceforth be directed into savings and finance (see Figure-1, F3). These units of surplus value are usually distributed to the holders of capital within the private company (i.e. shareholders).

Private companies are likely to develop and expand more easily if these units of surplus value are reintegrated within the internal company structure as a supplementary force (through self-financing). All that needs to occur is that the company's products are sold at a progressively higher price, which, of course, then results in inflation. The latter is, above all, deleterious to the interests of lenders (see "Suspect Money"); repayments being calculable in relation to the prevailing value of the currency at any given moment in time[12]. These units of surplus value can also accrue as a result of improvements in internal organization, or as a result of gains in productivity due to an improved yield from the labor force (hourly productivity rate). Moreover, the product itself is also capable of being transformed such that margins on its sale can be expanded accordingly. In such cases, it is the consumer who bears the brunt of the consequences. This new surplus decreed by the producer is no longer indexed to the numerical value of the basic labor materialized in the product but rather to the **purely nominal financial value of the money exchanged, the latter feeding upon itself in tandem with the values of the merchandise exchanged.** The principal actor, the worker-consumer, is neither owner of the productive resources in play, nor ultimately of his own salary. As a consequence, he is barely possessed of the means[13] to maintain his own purchasing

---

[12] All of which explains the permanent pressure from the actors concerned to diminish growth as much as possible.

[13] These are links of subordination inscribed within the very code of labor itself. This is the key to liberalism. Only the pressure exerted through strikes can enable any compensation. Moreover, should the latter exceed the level of losses accruing within the monetary volume allocated to wages, the drawback of inflation (trenchantly predicted by the ultra-liberals) will only impact upon lenders. This was certainly the case during the years of prosperity in France after the Second World War (*Les Trente Glorieuses*), during which purchasing power kept on increasing progressively without any reverse. This is also the case in developing nations enjoying a high growth rate. One might also note that the indexing of minimum-wage salaries in terms of the

power, his rate of pay being determined by the producer-owner.

The surplus which transits the potential inherent within supplementary units of value is thus dispersed beyond the boundaries of the private company. Accordingly, money is accumulated as capital. Indeed, only the State, the principal creator of money, is capable of controlling its use and importance through taxation and wage-control policies (such as the minimum wage, public assistance and diverse forms of income support, public-sector salaries, etc.).

Chief among the afflictions denounced by Marx are worker frustration and alienation. These can be seen as integral features of a system in which the means of redistribution are not at the disposal of Man-machine: the workers. Rather, these means continue to inhere in the tools themselves. Thus, the forces in motion, the very acts of purchasing which serve to impel the economic system forward, elude the control of the workers to the extent that it is not they who attribute value to their own products.

Within the system of liberal capitalism depreciation in the value of the products distributed in the consumer market is widely anticipated by producers and distributors alike, as well as financiers; such losses in value are compensated for by price rises which are

inflation rate in part facilitates the maintenance of a mean degree of purchasing power thanks to the knock-on effect within higher-salary bands.

accordingly added onto the basic surplus value accruing to the owner-producer. It is, of course, the purchasers, functioning as passive partners in the exchange, who bear the brunt of these re-evaluations. They are thus two-fold losers in the whole process: firstly, as we have already seen, in terms of the value expropriated from their work and, secondly, in terms of the general exploitation they submit to at the hands of financial institutions.

Crises

Owner-producers, in their desire to profit to excess from their financial advantages, always end up doing so to the detriment of production. Indeed, without the boost of a sufficient monetary return within the circuit of production, the latter can decline significantly. The most frequent case of this occurs when demand is saturated. Moreover, such situations have a tendency to degenerate through a chain of unintended consequences into fully-blown financial crises involving significant loss of liquidity. All of the interested parties will suffer the consequences of these crises in some way or another. Firstly, the worker-producer whose services are no longer required. Accordingly, the phenomenon of unemployment (viewed as an adjustment variable) can be explained, first and foremost, as the result of **monetary contraction.** Furthermore, the effects of such contraction can only be effectively mitigated by those parties possessing the greatest reserves. Conversely, the less-privileged classes will bear the brunt of the loss of revenue accruing from production; their precarious financial situation compounded by the pervasive threat to their employment prospects (and the effective blackmail which can be exercised upon them at the negotiating table as a result of this). These problems are further aggravated by that of excessive debt. In such situations, even the middle classes, fearful for their future, become reluctant to take out credit. Such reluctance will in turn inevitably impact upon banking operations, too, despite the countervailing attraction of low interest rates. This counter-weight to the contraction in the demand for credit is, of course, premised upon the intervention of the State through the offices of a Central Bank. When the demand for credit (and with it consumer demand) does pick up, this usually occurs first of all in the semi-durable goods market, in the market for cars for example, as well as the durable goods market exemplified by real estate. Ultimately, however, this momentum will only gather pace if state intervention occurs in time.

Conversely, excesses in the supply side of the economy are likely to generate crises of over-production, projected supply no longer tallying with prevailing demand. Indeed, this is exactly what occurred during the 'sub-prime' crisis of 2008 in the U.S.A, with over-production in the real-estate sector having induced a structural disparity between the level of production solicited by prevailing demand, on the one hand, and the purchasing power of the real-estate buyers targeted, on the other. Whatever the case, in order to avoid such generalized crises, whether their origin be material or financial, the regularity of monetary circulation needs to be ensured. In order for this to occur, a working equilibrium needs to be established between the various monetary volumes sustaining economic activity in general, including the payment of wages, the activities of the State, and the workings of the financial institutions. Accordingly, any emerging deficiency in the operative volume of liquidity requires immediate remedial compensation if the onset of systemic disequilibrium is to be avoided.

One might easily deduce from all this that any kind of error on the part of the State when allocating public money (in the name of budgetary rigor, for example) will automatically bring about a contraction in growth; similarly dysfunctional contractions might issue from a decline in the monetary volume allocated to wages and salaries (a concomitant of unemployment), or perhaps a reflex reluctance on the part of lenders to inject the necessary liquidity into the economy at any given moment. The corresponding pressure to decrease expenditure (otherwise known as *austerity*) will in turn trigger a decrease in the rate of overall economic growth, bringing in its wake a vicious deflationary spiral. Venture-capital operators can then set about buying up companies, buildings, and even public services at discount prices, secure in the knowledge that the value of these items will rise again once fresh liquidity has been injected into the system. This kind of speculative arbitrage on macro goods was seen flagrantly during the *coup d'état* in Chile (see Naomi Klein, *The Shock Strategy*). It also seems to be operating at the present time in Greece (2013-4), as can be clearly seen by the tenor of the discussions regarding national railway privatization. These kinds of strong-arm negotiating tactics were also in evidence in Argentina a decade ago; fortunately, the Argentinians were able to put up a difficult but nevertheless ultimately successful resistance in the face of pressure from the international banking community (regarding sovereign debt); they effectively achieved this by retrenching upon their own resources, counting only upon themselves.

Private companies on their last legs often have little choice but to sell themselves off to larger companies in the event of crisis, the latter being less critically affected than the former. In the wake of such operations, capitalism will undoubtedly have been able to strengthen its own powers. Taking a general perspective, the only way out of such an impasse is through the restoration of confidence in a future in which real hope can be invested: in concrete terms, through the engineering of a sustainable increase in purchasing power among the lower and middle classes, these classes comprising the majority of the population. Indeed, it is precisely these classes who enjoy the least opportunity to save and are thus least likely to remove an important percentage of liquidity from the system of production. Theoretically, the State also has the means to intervene through top-down monetary creation such as that effected by the imposition of a minimum wage.

FINANCIAL CAPITALISM

Financial capitalism is thus an avatar of productive capitalism. It represents a secondary effect of the system; one, moreover, which does not appear in its initial stages but, rather, is generated through an accumulation of factors. Indeed, this kind of capitalism only began to appear once a certain degree of wealth had been accumulated by the factory bosses during the process of industrialization. Financial capitalism was thus essentially created by the growing importance of monetary volumes in the whole process. Accordingly, the banks introduced themselves into this new monetary system, particularly during the early 19th century as the institution of the Stock Exchange began to establish itself. These Stock Exchanges effectively served as a meeting place for the new breed of investor-speculators who plunged their capital resources into grand industrial development projects. The Stock Exchange thus became a veritable temple of speculation; more or less predatory depending upon how gains accruing therein were re-employed and to what ends. This was seen, for example, at the time of OPA (*Offre*

64

public d'achats), which enabled private companies to increase their size, often through restructuring projects which were deleterious to the interests of those employees considered to be surplus to requirements.

The intrinsic power of money certainly existed at that time when it was represented in a material form other than symbolic figures printed on paper. However, the wealth generated only increased progressively to a certain degree, its scale limited by the time is took to undertake the transaction, and also the slow and difficult transportation of the metallic coin through which these transactions were mediated. Furthermore, the disappearance of tolls and other border controls meant that there was a need for significantly greater amounts of monetary volume in order to cater for the new markets springing up in response. The manufacture of metal coin was destined sooner or later to be replaced by bills which were representative of the same values but nevertheless much lighter. The increase in the geographical scope of individual markets thus became something of an ineluctable process as Man sought to meet his basic needs on an ever wider scale. Exchanges became ever more numerous and ever more remote from one another as Man reconciled himself to the inevitability that not everything could be produced locally. This process of expansion brought further benefits for the Economy, too, in the form of economies of scale. As monetary circulation expanded ever more rapidly, money itself became increasingly scriptural in form, all of which prefigured the disappearance of cash forms in favor of numerical transactional devices.

The banks which controlled monetary circulation took full advantage of this in order to exploit a significant portion of the cash flows which passed into their accounts. The initial exploitation consisted of short-term loans subsidizing the purchase of consumer durables for those whose revenues did not otherwise allow immediate acquisition of such goods. It is important to bear in mind that this kind of loan to private individuals only became general practice after the Second World War[14], notably in relation to the financing of semi-durable markets such as that of the car, and durables such as real estate. For the entrepreneurs, it became a matter of securing the tools enabling them to quickly pay off their debts as well as to stack up their profits. These kinds of acquisition represented efficient acts of speculation to the extent that they seemed to promise a future full of 'promise'. In periods of productive growth, the circulation of monetary volumes became more rapid; these monetary volumes were themselves boosted by the supplementary gains on interest accruing. This system of financial capitalism in turn generates its

---

14 This was significantly facilitated by the second Basel agreement between the banks which authorized banks to lend money which they themselves had borrowed in the wholesale markets. This was conditional upon a stipulated capital reserve of 8%..

own side-effects, these being due to its own inherent mode of development: markets generating wealth which boosts the markets which generate wealth in a permanently virtuous cycle. Concomitantly, general wealth also increases; however, this is likely to remain badly distributed[15] unless the State intervenes through various forms of aid. The absence of employment contributions (effectively forms of differed salary) lead to similar distortions in the distribution of income.

From these reflections we can draw a very firm conclusion: that purchasing power should imperatively be either maintained or increased in correlative terms such that it functions as the principal direct economic driver maintaining the equilibrium of the system. Moreover, this prioritizing of demand-driven economic policy should occur freely without undue attention being paid to the dangers of inflation (a necessary concomitant of the accompanying price rises).

This system of circular forces in motion is possessed of an extraordinary power, as indeed is any tool of this kind: that of transmitting the energy which Man draws from the earth. This energy, of course, issues ultimately from the Big Bang, enabling Man to obtain the products necessary to his survival. These products have been at the disposal of Man since his emergence on earth, progressively

---

15 Total redistribution remains a myth which has been thoroughly institutionalized under the name of *ruissellement* ("trickle down effect') in France.

accumulated and reinforced by new tools which accordingly strengthen his purchase upon the environment. This represents the very basis of material progress[16] itself, a progress which latterly has extended to the attainment of considerable comfort for certain categories of the population, an ease which often spills over into material surfeit.

This particular effect only makes itself manifest in the long term; it will only be sustained or increased if the demand for goods is itself sustained by a stable or expanding demographic base, or if the various markets concerned are themselves sufficiently sustained by the availability of cash for purchases. Therein lies a pertinent explanation for the relative disappearance of the value of labour: as soon as the latter becomes mediated by monetary exchange, it can end up serving little other end than the creation of speculative bubbles, the latter in turn often blown up to an inordinate degree by the effect of monetary drag. Its initial unitary value (which Marx referred to as the value of use) thus becomes negligible in relation to the wealth accumulated over time through the cause-and-effect operations of the double system: the result of labour and the products issuing therefrom, which in turn feed back into monetary flows. All of which corroborates our postulate that the labor-product relationship which lies at the very heart of the production process itself becomes doubly corrupted at source as soon as it

---

16 To the detriment of natural resources as long as energy remains necessary to material production.

enters into the cash nexus: by virtue of the surplus value generated through margins accruing from labour (as Marx again identified), and thus ultimately by virtue of the **agency of money itself.** This point lies at the very crux of the thesis I wish to expound here.

The predatory power of financial capitalism.

This aspect of things certainly had not escaped the attention of J.M. Keynes either, as was evident when he drew the important distinction between productive capitalism, on the one hand, and financial capitalism, on the other. According to the Keynesian view of things, the latter should be analyzed at the very moment of its emergence, as a tool enabling private companies to develop and expand. This particular understanding of macro-economics is well worth retaining as it will enable us to establish a more refined understanding of the role of money within the dynamic of financial flows, as well as the fluctuations in interest rates which are closely linked to this monetary agency, representing determinable side-effects of the latter. Money has thus become indispensable as the operating force within these systems in motion. Moreover, each of the constitutive systems generates unwanted side-effects, corrosion and waste, respectively.

As we have seen, the owners of the tools of production set themselves up so that these surplus values can be readily appropriated as soon as they emerge. These surplus values thus represent an important component in the overall generation of wealth, with the rest to be filtered back down to the workforce in the form of wages. **Moreover, these distortions in the redistribution of wealth serve as an important brake on overall economic activity.** As a result of the latter, economic crises and sharp rises in the rate of unemployment are likely to ensue as the rate of production dips in response to diminishing purchasing power[17]. This dynamic is a pernicious one for as soon as unemployment sets in as an endemic feature of the economy, purchasing power will decrease concomitantly, thus setting in motion a predatory vicious circle which is difficult to arrest. The hiving off of funds which have been capitalized in this way, when factored into the system in tandem with gains in productivity, lies at the root of the phenomenon of mass unemployment. It is thus the holders of capital who

---

17 There are two kinds of speculation: firstly, that which is undertaken with a view to increasing the forces of production; secondly, that which is undertaken with a view to enriching those who undertake it (the latter being, by definition, predatory). Financiers thus furnish a fictive boost to 'purchasing power' through the agency of credit. However, this system – an inordinately powerful tool entirely due to the establishment of time-saving devices – is a variable one. Indeed, it can even represent a source of potential disaster if the purchasing power of the borrowers is too weak to guarantee reliable repayments. This was patently the case in the recent 'Sub-prime' crisis.

should be held ultimately responsible for this scourge[18].

Predatory agency thus remains latent but nevertheless effective within the money accumulated through financial capitalism, the latter having outgrown the power of productive capitalism. This latent predatory agency can be explained by the progressive falsification of primary monetary values incurred as the latter circulate and shift their initial domain of attribution. These displacements serve to skew the whole mechanism of value attribution operated by money. As the latter becomes more and more remote from the initial value accruing from labour, any natural restraints upon its expansion are thus progressively removed. The near fatal danger of all this irrationality is plain for all to see, with crisis following upon crisis within those human societies founded upon the apparent 'verity' of free markets.

Supply-side strategies are articulated with demand-boosting incentives which impact upon purchasing decisions (see Keynes Figure 23). It is precisely for this reason that subsidies given to private companies from the State tend to be received as windfalls, largely inefficient ones at that in terms of their impact upon overall development given that these incentives do not always completely satisfy the real needs of consumers. The leverage effect operated by the reinvestment of money within the private company is thus no longer

18 See the notions of competition and greed denounced by Joseph Stieglitz. (*The Triumph of Greed*).

guaranteed. This is the essence of the risk incurred by the establishment of free-market liberalism. When investments are inefficiently directed, it is the private company which suffers in the form of poor results, these in turn leading to lay-offs in the final analysis. From all this, we can see how the financial system effectively creams off the wealth generated by productive margins accruing from labour, with the private banks coming to establish themselves as indispensable intermediaries. This wealth is preserved in the form of property guaranteed by money, only to be ceaselessly re-capitalized within a system dictated by the laws of competition between individual private companies within a free market.

This deviated monetary wealth seized by the financiers serves as a brutal index of the perversity inherent within the whole system; this is encapsulated by the fact that these financiers can effectively enrich themselves without working [19]. Moreover, this remains a state of affairs that 'pragmatic' monetarists are happy to declare as normal and natural. The problem with all this is that the norm within a state of nature is rarely anything more than dog eat dog!

In this way, we can begin to explain how competition between private companies comes to be distorted by the mere contribution of money, the most powerful among these going as far as to absorb the human and material capital of their weaker

---

19 We can concur here with Keynes regarding the rentier class and euthanasia!

counterparts. *A fortiori* with respect to multinationals.

BOX-4: Predicting the Economy.

It is impossible to produce reliable predictive models as the efficiency of any given system can only be proven *a posteriori.* Statistical facts pertaining to the Economy only confer a sense upon it retrospectively after its composite modes of functioning have generated their various effects. In this respect, any prescriptive inferences regarding desirable ends can only be made on a probabilistic basis. Empirical models, whatever their structure might be, enable econometric analysts to recommend certain controls and rectifications in the short term. These, of course, will be contingent upon the complexity and the speed of the developments under analysis.

Systems embody objectives which give rise to directions foreseen in the original program, albeit without prejudging the results, these remaining open to influence during the unfolding of the process. These conceptualizations being contingent, the material and intellectual results emerge from a dialectic, the final consequences of which are likely to remain open to chance.

By framing this problematic uniquely in terms of 'how' the proposed models function, empirical researchers effectively leave political responsibility in the hands of the politicians regarding which predictive economic model to act upon.

The Politics of the Economy.
How monetarism came to propagate the power of predatory money.

Man has always known how to exploit that other natural tool: his native intelligence. Indeed, it is very much thanks to this mechanism of self-defence that he was able to avert his own rapid extinction, having become particularly vulnerable in a hostile world. Are we now once again faced with a turning point of similar magnitude? To what extent might a reasoned awareness of the kind of risks that we have been assessing enable Man to eventually mitigate the predatory effects of the ultra-liberal exchange system in which he has become mired? How might the most tangible and nefarious consequences be avoided in the long term? As regards the numerous directors and economists who remain strongly wedded to empirical models based upon accountancy, supposedly rational by virtue of their mathematical tenor, have they become blinded as a result of their own interest in maintaining existing inequalities in the distribution of wealth? Conversely, might humanitarian directors or economists who find themselves operating outside the existing political system be able to show how the situation might be taken in hand? Might these 'outsiders' be able to modify certain parameters of the situation, re-orientating it toward a less dramatic consummation than that predicted by many?

As we know, every kind of tool represents in itself a discrete system which serves to modify a given state; in doing so, generating at least one, and often several, side effects. Money has been a veritably double-edged sword in human affairs: on the one hand, it has acted as a prime driver in the development of human affairs; on the other, it remains responsible for the litany of horrors that have spanned this historical development. Although recognizing the importance of the functioning of the monetary system, the philosophy promoted by the 'Chicago' monetarist school considers that such effects cannot be effectively controlled by the exercise of political agency in any respect, regardless of the negative consequences that might eventually be entailed by the untrammeled operation of the 'laws" governing the free market.

The chances of satisfying demand will always remain subject to prevailing contingencies; the latter a function of the will of the mass of purchasers. Moreover, this will can be seen as being strongly contingent in turn upon current, and above all future, purchasing power, and thus upon the consumer confidence that can be projected therefrom. This psychological aspect of mass behaviour (see the diagram in Figure-2: "psychological pressure on monetary circulation"; see also box 2, "The functioning of systems") **is a founding element of the economy in that it determines the act of purchase.**

Production supply is in fact becoming less and less material. In these conditions, it matters little if growth is infinite as it is monetary creation and its rotation which creates new wealth by virtue of the self-generating growth inherent therein. Indeed, it is worth stressing that full employment can be guaranteed in the long term provided that the State governs the constitutive flows of the system wisely. Of course, for this to occur, there needs to be a sufficient number of acts of purchase in relation to a given volume of production: in general the volume of production released onto the market presupposes a certain projected level of demand synchronized across the whole spectrum of the consumer population. In this way, supply and demand will be brought into a projected concordance with one another. The following point is absolutely crucial to our thesis: i.e. that the private company can in no way be seen as the originator of growth, nor indeed of job creation. Rather, this role devolves upon the "consumer", the purchaser in all of his guises, whatever the product might be.

Even if the State successfully manages to guarantee the value of the national currency (by printing its own coin), it cannot, for all that, necessarily control the range of unintended side effects perversely undermining its value. From these warning signs we can begin to apprehend, once a certain critical threshold has been passed, the risk of a state of chronic disequilibrium emerging between the financial sector (which remains unregulated in the majority of Western economies), on the one hand, and that of productive capitalism, on the other. Money is a system which, as such, is incapable of restoring equilibrium through the workings of its own internal dynamic alone unless new forces compensating for the loss of monetary volumes incurred during periods of recession are introduced. In order to preempt the possibility of any new break-up of the system, monetary flows need to be kept in circulation. It is precisely this imperative which can be adduced to explain the recent bank bail-outs following the dramatic losses of liquidity suffered by the latter. These were, fortunately, enough to keep the economies concerned going on a basic operative level However, given that these new injections of liquidity were only compensatory devices, the recovery in economic activity continued to be thwarted. Moreover, in such cases, other accidents can also occur. All of which might be elucidated by the following analogy: if one gives Nature a free hand in economic affairs, one is always likely to run the risk of a heart attack!

Figure 3
EMPLOYMENT

THE RATE OF EMPLOYMENT VARIES
IN RELATION TO THE ROTATIVE
FORCES IN ACTION
(The balance on foreign trade impacts either
positively or negatively on the rate of
employment by acting on monetary force)

WORK productions
forces including
services

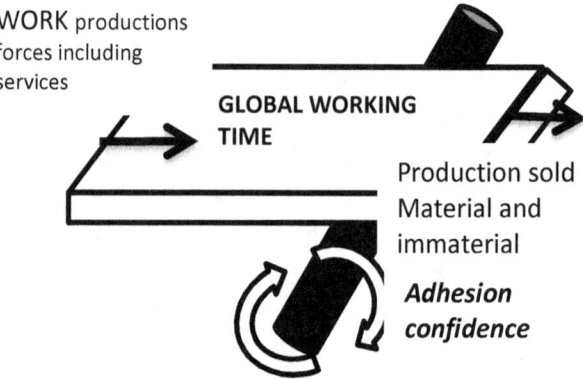

GLOBAL WORKING
TIME

Production sold
Material and
immaterial

*Adhesion
confidence*

Rotative monetary force
(purchase circulation)

What next for employment?

Interest indexed to currency impacts negatively upon employment, the latter already undermined by the effect of the surplus value extracted therefrom. Monetary volumes issuing from rent and that flowing through wages tend to pull the economy in opposite directions, generating diametrically opposed objectives: in the first case, minimize outlay on salary, replacing any earnings deficit by a value to be recovered in the long-term by the lender. Conversely, wage earners seek to increase their real purchasing power in the here and now, even if they lack the apparent wherewithal to do so. Indeed, it is the calculated exploitation of this disparity in real time by banks and private companies which enables these parties to profit from the system.

The activity of a given national economy can be redirected in favour of job creation (or otherwise, as the case may be). Moreover, job creation represents a fundamental economic driver as well as catering for a primary anthropological need. All that is required is to master the process whereby money is created and then to monitor the way in which it is redistributed in order to control economic activity, and thus growth, and thus employment.

This kind of market activity constantly increases in the long term (numerically indexed as growth in the Gross National Product figures). This is not immediately reflected by any correlative increase in the productive workforce, however. This stalling in economic development can be attributed to lags in the replacement of active human labour by tools and automated machinery. This is pertinently exemplified by the recent computerization of modern working practices. The lags involved here are almost impossible to calculate; nevertheless, one can confidently affirm from any perspective that the benefits accruing in terms of growth and general economic activity have been considerable, with new wealth and employment generated afresh in their wake. These benefits remain contingent, of course, upon the eventual elimination of the initial lags thwarting progress.

The State has at its disposal the means to compensate for the negative consequences of any slow-down. Principally, these means are comprised of productive investments in non-privatized sectors as well as the all-important public funds allocated through income support and other financial breaks directed at the spending sector of the population. The principal vectors of such expenditure include: family income support, national education, bonuses, and, above all, public-sector salaries. At this point, it would be well worth reminding ourselves that it is the masses who constitute the very heart and soul of economy activity by virtue of their serial acts of purchase[20]. Not, it might be added, the private

---

20 Both *activity* and *acts* bear the same etymological derivation, cognate with *action.*

company, as one would have had us believe now for decades! The idea that private companies 'create employment' is little more than a pernicious fallacy at the end of the day. Rather, functioning as intermediaries (albeit indispensable ones given that they own the means of production), all they effectively do is to hire and fire on an anticipatory basis in response to the pressure of prevailing demand. It is the latter, of course, which represents the true source of job creation. It is well worth underlining a further, and corollary, point: that it is not the **results** declared in the budget which, whether the latter is balanced or not, lie at the origin of this activity, but rather exclusively **expenditure** of the kind that I have alluded to (above). Moreover, this is precisely what Keynes himself advocated. Accordingly, the whole enterprise of chasing after the chimera of deficit management becomes a futile, not to say utterly absurd, one. Indeed, more often than not, these deficits can be seen as little more than the product of circumstances and are liable to be canceled naturally once given investments have been brought to fruition. Indeed, to paraphrase the all-too-relevant dictum of Adam Smith: One does not manage the economy of a country as one manages a household budget.

At the present time, the banks, holding exclusive purview over the accounts of both producers and consumers, are the sole agents capable of knowing where money comes from and wither it departs. Indeed, it would be no easy task to verify their own accounts against a dizzying contemporary backdrop of speculative investment and increasingly rapid monetary flows. Moreover, an account only offers a momentary (and thus provisional) snapshot of monetary volumes in circulation; it is a vector through which money is reserved and released. The only way of controlling these movements would be to draw a distinction between different kinds of currency in relation to their origin and their destination. In this way, we might in turn be able to draw clear analytical distinctions regarding their use (as we have seen in the previous chapter). Furthermore, by drawing a clear corollary distinction between the value of the currency as linked to the productive system, on the one hand, and that linked to the financial system, on the other, it is to be hoped that a significant degree of control might be exercised over the general articulation of these two systems in tandem motion. The proliferating hydra of neo-liberal economics might thus be brought to bay through a concerted act of knowledge, one enabling a just recognition of the relevant transactional monetary values in circulation.

By this means, it would become possible to draw pertinent distinctions about financial actions in relation to whether they served purely speculative and predatory ends or whether they served to boost investment and thereby production. Indeed, it is worth pointing out that the much-touted separation of investment banking from retail banking advocated by certain economists will remain a strict impossibility without a clear delimitation of two currencies. However, provided that they remained clearly separate and discretely articulated, all of these flows in motion could be easily managed by information systems operating within the banks themselves[21]. If this technique were to be adopted by those in power, this would enable decision-makers to boost economic activity by redirecting the result of its constitutive operating practices toward the sector of work, all of which would have tangible benefits for the employment rate. Economic crises and unemployment are always linked!

The distinction drawn above represents a proposition in relation to the national economy of France: to establish a specifically financial currency such as the *Ecu*, with the *Franc* in turn becoming the currency used in primary markets.

Exercising control over bank circuits would enable our governors to recognize and distribute those goods in common circulation in accordance with the level of demand prevailing in the real economy. Financial goods pertaining to the banking sector might be similarly ascertained[22]. Switches

---

21 This is outlined in my French publication *En finir avec les crises et le chomage,* 'Domestiquer le finance'. This demonstration is graphically presented in Figure-1 'Flux monétaires des quatres acteurs économiques'. From this demonstration, we can readily infer the sub-title *A la conquête du plein emploi.*

22 After the Second World War, banks were nationalized in France, which enabled the State to control and monitor

would be made from one currency to another in accordance with the requirements of the situation (purchases, loans). These switches would be materialized, aggregated, and filtered according to the contingencies of the moment and in relation to a rate of exchange determined by the State, as indeed occurs with currency exchanges executed across national borders.

In the liberal State, private finance would thus be able to remain present as a powerful source of liquidity fructifying the Economy.

GROWTH AND EVOLUTION

Redistribution of wealth occurs on the basis of surplus values generated during the process of production. As long as the role of Man has not been completely supplanted within the Economy, this redistribution is likely to remain unequal. However, this is unlikely ever to happen. Increases in productive output, whether of a material or spiritual nature, generally entail a concomitant increase in the number of tools used in the production process (this entailment is frequently referred to as the boomerang effect). *Concomitantly, new human needs will be created as a result of the requirement*

---

credit. From this period issued a period of unrivaled prosperity (known in France as *Les Trente Glorieuses*): finances were, in the main, directed toward production. In the 1970s, however, the French State began to disengage itself from such *dirigiste* policies, supposedly in order to mount the battle against inflation.

to administratively manage, whether publicly or privately, the new production techniques which have come into operation as the manufacturing process is refined and perfected, constantly generating new systems in the process. Progressively greater quantities of information also come to be processed as a result of such progress, thus in turn rendering the production process all the more complex and sophisticated: control and surveillance become indispensable adjuncts in these new organizational systems, these undergoing barely perceptible but nevertheless significant changes in quality. Moreover, any system which shows the slightest permeability to the environment will require adaptive adjustment thereto. Inevitably, certain items of information, certain unforeseen empirical events, will remain unprocessed by the systems in operation. All of which gives rise to predictable dysfunctional errors, these in turn necessitating the intervention of Man in order to correct them. In doing so, he will also create new systems of life.

All of the problems encountered by the current ultra-liberal economic system stem from the fact that the base metal dematerialized by its written representation in the form of notes[23] (and *a fortiori* in purely scriptural form as bank accounts) has effectively become abstracted from its material consistency and base. The monetary system

---

23 In fact, since the failed attempt of the

functions in a permanently cyclical way, impelled by monetary creation. Indeed, the phenomenal increase in the monetary volumes in circulation means that little else but fully-blown crises can slow this progression down. Within the economic system, Money thus becomes effectively autonomous; driven by the power of labor (whether physical or intellectual), it perpetuates itself in a trajectory progressively dilated by its own movement. It is certainly true that the power of Money was already manifest at the time when minted coin was all that passed muster; however, productive wealth only increased progressively on a scale considerably reduced in relation to the time taken to carry out transactions as well as that involved in the often arduous and difficult transportation of important sums. In the light of these difficulties, the appearance of paper notes became something of an inevitability as a result of the development of wide-ranging markets and the concomitant disappearance of tolls and other border controls of this nature. The banks, in their capacity as expert accountants and intermediaries, also became an indispensable cog in the machinery of circulation driving monetary volumes of ever increasing value, these volumes being transmitted from one banking haven to another.

This kind of systemic understanding of affairs can even be found in colloquial idioms and proverbs such as: *time is money* and *money goes where money is.* In principle, of course, Money tends to go to private companies and financial institutions before it goes anywhere else. Moreover, within a given system, time is effectively the element which can cause certain movements to become uncontrolled in their orientation. Accordingly, it is thus in relation to other parameters, such as the origin and the destination of information programmed by the actors themselves, that any degree of control becomes possible, if only to the extent that a certain portion can be channeled and then redistributed individually in the most egalitarian way possible. Any given movement is effectively a vector, and thus constitutes a directed force. The State has the means at its disposal to modify these directions in that it controls the printing as well as the collection and re-injection of liquidity into the economic system by means of the budget.

We have almost arrived at the end of our study of the mechanical Economy. In doing so, we have kept firmly in view the psychological aspect involved in the behavior of its principal actors as well as that of the general mass of the population itself, those responsible for consumption. We have seen that the perverse side-effects generated by a money-system liberated from its material base. These side effects manifest themselves within a purely social domain, bringing both beneficial development (i.e. investment) as well as more predatory tendencies to the fore once a certain threshold of volume in motion has been crossed. Any degree of control only becomes possible if one is able to inventory monetary movements in accordance with a specified value and orientation, calculated in terms of the origin and destination designated by their trajectory. For example, in France, the *Ecu* would become a specific notational currency in relation to these inventoried movements. This initially financial currency would then be converted into francs by virtue of a filtering process conducted within the banks themselves. It could thus be used as a controlling mechanism in relation to the deceleration of the constitutive flows driving the Economy. The precise degree of deceleration would be determined by the destination of the flows: loans, investments, purchases.

As I have already suggested, the immaterial needs of *homo sapiens* require satisfaction as much as his material needs. These immaterial needs coalesce in the various realms of his spiritual aspiration; in pleasure, in love, in art, in the theater, in general culture, in leisure, health, and in all the diverse spheres which enable Man to transcend his own condition. Indeed, it is by no means a coincidence that **producers** also exist in these spheres. Any kind of growth in production mechanically entails a corresponding growth in the number of productive (or administrative) workers. Moreover, new forms of labor linked to the growth of the new information sectors can also be easily foreseen; these sectors, too, will require their controllers, managers and administrators.

How many new forms of employment in this domain will be linked to television? All of the public and private domains developed to manage the realities of everyday life are now developing into progressively more complex forms; accordingly, it may become necessary to find specialists, workers trained in new disciplinary fields, in order to deal with the side- effects of such growing complexity. Indeed, in such cases, it would be entirely reasonable to apply the same rules as those encountered when analyzing material production; circulating currency acting as a vehicle for the exchange of material goods can also be used to quantify any kind of value generated by dint of human labor. In any case, there will always be the risk that certain merchandised values will go beyond a certain threshold of monetary volume, thus producing deleterious social reflexes on a mass scale. This threat of dysfunctional behavior on a collective scale inevitably brings in its wake measures of control.

If it is possible to determine the cost of immaterial values produced, conversely, it is impossible to quantify the degree of satisfaction experienced by their consumers to any precise degree. This impossibility stems from the fact that such satisfaction is by definition totally subjective. This kind of need to satisfy is effectively boundless, as is the imagination of the producers who come to the fore to fulfill it. Indeed, we know all too well that the value of services accounted for in Gross National Product is increasingly comprised of the production figures relating to immaterial goods. Moreover, this trend is occurring at the expense of those relating to material goods, which are declining in both relative and absolute terms. In the need for material protection, catered for by the housing market for example, we also need to include personal care. In the need for communication (as manifested, for example, in physical transport) we also need to include the transmission of universal and commonly-shared social values.

However, the satisfaction of physical needs also comes at a price. The volume of monetary circulation thus generated increases ineluctably, tending to take over the baton from material production, the latter having risen to inordinate dimensions in our Western countries. This is also borne out in contemporary figures for growth, which should in principle create new employment in an almost mechanical relationship of cause and effect. If this were to be the case, then growth should indeed always be prioritized, *pace* the anti-growth strictures of the modern ecological movement, who tend to focus exclusively upon the excesses of material production at the expense of other kinds (such as those that we have mentioned above). Moreover, it is worth noting that this new kind of currency has barely any need of natural resources and circulates without generating undue side-effects in the environment.

Supply-side economic policies function by incentivizing producers (see Figure-2); the political cursor has effectively been directed toward private enterprise for a considerable period of time now. This remains a fundamental tenet of the ultra-liberal doctrine which continues to inform the decision-making process at the very highest levels of world economic policy. Moreover, the enduring prevalence of such priorities can be adduced to explain the frequent derailing of the economic (and thus the social) machine whenever recession strikes. These crises will occur whenever monetary flows do not act in concert to produce growth. On the other hand, demand-driven policies are orientated in priority toward the satisfaction of real needs. As J.M. Keynes consistently advocated, expenditure should be prioritized at all costs because it operates directly upon the Economy; it is thereby more psychologically efficient as long as confidence prevails in all key sectors thereof. Indeed, the only way in which full employment can be assured is by maintaining the requisite degree of constantly regulated economic growth, fostered both by flows issuing from a healthy demand (on the part of consumers), on the one hand, and then complemented by those from the supply-side of the Economy (i.e. from the private sector and from financial institutions), on the other. Ensuring growth by controlling[24] its sources in this way represents the only way to guarantee progress, provided, of course, that the financial institutions do not manipulate these techniques to their own advantage.

The Economy is nothing more or less than the socialized form of the evolutionary process. It is precisely for this reason that we cannot really explain why (and at what time) fundamental change in any given system occurred when it appeared to be functioning perfectly well of its own accord, unhindered by any apparent obstacle. In the same way, we do not really know when or why a new species of animal appeared when it did. Another well-known effect of economic and social evolution is the emergence of a discretely quantitative domain, the latter in turn retroactively transforming the domain of the qualitative once a certain threshold has been crossed. A range of qualitative effects manifests itself at a certain quantitative level as soon as one manages to formally categorize an integrated set of objects. One might compare this, albeit in terms of a reverse series of effects, to the process known under the name of the *butterfly effect*. Qualitative change is creation!

The passage from the quantitative to the qualitative pertains to the domain of perception, and

---

24 This control would be exercised according to its qualitative contents, in favor of ecology and the environment. All of which it is possible to carry out by virtue of taxation and incentivizing pricing policies (such as the *bonus-malus* in France).

thus to the very origins of humanity itself. In this respect, it remains resolutely incompatible with statistical methods of analysis (see Box-4). Quality is an aspect of the social economy which eludes quantitative determination, although, rather paradoxically, it can also be seen to depend upon the latter. How many grains of sand would be needed before one would be in a position to claim that one had a fistful of sand in one's hand? This kind of evaluation is destined to remain strictly approximate. By the same token, we cannot really explain why and at precisely what time a given qualitative change took place on the basis of a particular statistical result in cases in which side effects have been accumulating and compounding for a certain period of time. The Economy seen in this way encourages us to take a certain distance from what has become the normative model for orthodox economists . According to this quantitative conception of matters, only the truth of figures counts under the pretext that a kilo of feathers is equivalent to that of a kilo of lead. And yet who would deny that being struck by a kilo of feathers is likely to be the less painful option! The living realism of Keynes' followers must surely be preferred to the numbing abstractions of the orthodoxy expounded so dogmatically by Anglophone monetarists under the cover of pragmatism. The **normal** macro-economy, when compared to the narrow little micro-economy of the small shop-keeper, only stands out in relation to the size of its budget.

Everything takes place as if the pressure imposed upon a given volume of objects could, once a certain threshold has been crossed, bring about a change in appearance. For example, modifying the size of a butterfly's wings in order to modify, if at all possible, the moment in which a future disequilibrium is likely to be triggered[25].

The diagram in Figure-2 shows that it is possible to act in favor of growth by controlling monetary circulation empirically, to the point of determining the investment of these monetary volumes in carefully-measured doses such that their impact might be significant, but without any of the excesses which might bring about a disturbance in the delicate equilibrium of internal pressures. In this way, it might become possible to counteract any deficits in the total volume of wages by means of budgetary measures. Indeed, this is precisely what Keynes himself advocated in relation to State spending, without concerning himself unduly with any potential deficits which might come in its wake. The prioritization of expenditure has also been advocated by Haavelmo[26]. The determination of the quantitative dose should also be calculated by taking into account what might represent the most propitious juncture for intervention within a system which is still developing and evolving. When it comes to investment the priority should be accorded in relation to the range of likely responses among

---

25 We might describe this as a kind of Darwinian effect.
26 Nobel Price winner in 1989.

key sectors of the economically-active population. The path taken by these monetary injections should also be the most direct one possible within given circumstances. In this way, the so-called 'Welfare' State might be able to increase its payments to the population at large and, above all, oblige the private sector to increase the lower wage band in accordance with a newly-determined minimum wage, even to the extent of dipping into its own budget in order to compensate for the costs incurred by these new measures. Moreover, an attractive range of credit from the banks is likely to follow on almost automatically from such measures. The three principal economic actors will thus be solicited in a selective but nevertheless harmonious order. Once the total volume of wages has been increased, renewed confidence within the population at large (the fourth and most important actor) will take care of the rest. Growth will be renewed and, as a natural consequence, a healthy level of employment restored.

As we have seen, the functioning of the Economy is thus by no means a purely mechanical affair. By the same token, applying human strength to the workings of a tool is dependent upon a set of decisions whose consequences will inevitably remain unclear. Ultimately, one can only hope that these consequences will match expectations. This is certainly the case as regards individual acts of speculation which are only likely to become predatory once a certain imprecise quantitative threshold has been crossed. This is also the case when production that has become excessive in a certain sector brings about crises of under- or over-production in its wake. *A fortiori* in the case of financial crises. How will consumers behave? How are they going to assess the general situation and what it implies for the prevailing rate of consumer confidence (Figure-3)? As suggested, we do not really know at what point a private company becomes decisively modified and, in changing its scale, thus changes its 'nature'. Indeed, it is precisely for this reason that J.M. Keynes concluded his study of the macro economy by acknowledging that it is likely to fluctuate in accordance with factors which are as much psychological as physical. All of which does not prevent us from taking logical decisions as regards monetary policy as these are, in principle, the only ones genuinely available[27]. Viewed from this perspective, ultra-liberalism is nothing more or less than the extension of the traditional liberal system, albeit bloated beyond any degree of restraint or control, against which Keynes himself directed his fire. Having crossed a decisive threshold of operation, the system changes qualitatively. Nevertheless, very little of tangible import has

---

27 Harmonious growth presupposes that the relevant actors inject liquidity into the system in the appropriate measures, at the most suitable time and place in order to avoid undue excesses in the circulation of liquidity or generally negative impact. Such measures are accordingly premised upon the implementation of suitable regulatory measures. which have been well adapted to the prevailing circumstances.

actually changed since the 1980's when the world of finance managed to persuade various governments to abandon Keynesian economics in favor of a supply-side monetarism which directly favored the interests of the banks and various lending institutions. In particular, lowering the inflation rate was prioritized above all else on the premise that it was damaging to the interests of the population at large, whereas it was, of course, above all fundamentally damaging to the interests of these financial institutions themselves[28]. In fact, all that was needed was that inflation remain at a mean rate sufficient to guarantee basic stability. Here, too, the importance of volumes plays an important role. There are certain thresholds beyond which one cannot go. Moreover, this risk becomes all the more pronounced in the case of the developing countries: it is naturally entailed by their strong growth. On the other hand, for the European countries, the risk is a low one. Accordingly, lowering inflation by blocking the printing of money by the State has had, as a direct consequence, the stifling of growth as well as the concomitant increase in sovereign debt and general budgetary deficits. And, of course, in its wake comes the most human consequence of all: mass unemployment. It would be no exaggeration to say that the creation of monetary volumes, and with it an important vehicle of state power, has been

---

28 Keynes himself suggested that Euthanasia might be a good
    solution for the *rentier* class!

effectively highjacked by the banks in their own interests.

Indeed, the whole economic chessboard has been transformed by the multiplication of monetary volumes to particularly high levels across the globe. Moreover, the various states of disequilibrium brought about by this globalization of monetary exchange means that the pursuit of an independent national economic policy becomes all the more problematic. Questions of vital importance remain: Do these huge flows of money pertain for the most part to productive capitalism or financial capitalism? How can they be mastered?

Why has the pace of Man's existence and evolution accelerated to such an inordinate degree over the past few centuries? Has this frenetic increase in pace come about as a result of or despite the role of Money that we have elucidated in this essay? What kind of time-scale might we plausibly project for any political attempt to control the predatory side effects which have accompanied its rise?

This dual heritage, violence and progress, constitutes nothing less than the permanent reality of monetarism. Little wonder, then, that it has sometimes found itself to be the target of denunciation from certain religions, i.e. Catholic, Jewish, and Muslim. Conversely, it has been thoroughly embraced by both Puritans (is this a coincidence?) and Anglophone pragmatists. Their apparent moral rigor has been appealed to in order to justify, thanks to the 'objectivity' of the figures adduced in support of this rigor, thanks to the tenets of a so-called realism, the only admissible economic truth: interest (in the two senses of the term) implying that one should not to neglect one's wealth and, indeed, even feel it to be entirely justified. According to this conception, Money would fall like a manna from heaven[29;] it would then be necessary to manage this manna in an economic way, through austerity measures predominantly, and if absolutely necessary by resort to force. Accordingly, it is to be considered as a gift bestowed by God, one which needs preserving and managing in all of its various states. It is thus necessary to let the manna come into one's possession, according to his Will, and without further intermediary agency. As for the predatory practices which ensue, these would be considered to be equally natural, and thus there would be no need to worry oneself unduly about the violence that each living species needs to generate from its own vital forces in order to guarantee survival in permanent competition with other species. Might these trenchant and apparently archetypical distinctions ultimately boil down, in historical terms, to the intransigence of the Lutherans pitted against the Classical tolerance advocated by Voltaire and his followers?

The anti-liberal Marxist solution aspired to do away with the predatory inequalities inherent in the

---

29 On dollar bills and coins, we find the motto "In God we trust".

old system, as was seen for example when the communist state in the U.R.S.S. abolished private ownership of the means of production. Despite these efforts, Money continued to circulate, albeit slowly. Nevertheless, its characteristically deviant side effects were still generated to a certain degree; those that found themselves placed within the circuits of monetary exchange set about seizing the meager resources generated therein. As a result of these developments, certain brakes came to slow down the production process, particularly given that the latter was badly managed due to the lack of practical administrative resources to be found in the central management agencies directing the Economy. Prices and salaries were centrally decreed; accordingly, individual creativity within the context of private enterprise was discouraged as the attraction of private monetary holdings became effectively redundant. Slowly, the system became eroded by the gangrene of corruption. At the same time, systemic weaknesses became endemic as the decelerating speed of monetary rotation lost its power to dynamize in the absence of private property. Ultimately, the whole system seemed destined to collapse around its own internal contradictions as the corrosion of its motions began to wear everything down without any compensatory momentum toward restoration.

Taking advantage of the failure of the Soviet system, Western liberals lost no time in adducing this failure as proof of the exclusive validity of their own system. Indeed, liberals had always been staunch opponents of the corruption of the Soviet system; when the walls finally came down, however, it was the ultra-liberals, and their excessive monetarist doctrines, who had come to rule the roost, bringing in their wake ever more debilitating recessions leading only to failure[30]. This pernicious

---

30 There would, of course, remain the possibility of the total suppression of monetary circulation. All that would be needed for this to occur would be that a uniquely scriptural Money be managed by means of a monetized card, budgeted according to the salaries of of workers who would in any case remain in any case modulated according to the needs and capacities of each individual. The mere abolition of private means of production were not sufficient. Accordingly, it would have been necessary to halt the circulation of money, a tool which can be used to measure value, keeping only the value of labor (as decreed) in order to buy given products without any financial value added on. Price-fixing would, of course, remain necessary, not so much as a gauge of the value of goods bought as a means of determining the amount of production which might be necessary at any given time in terms of a ratio ratio calculated on the basis of total purchases against unitary price. This kind of political economy, managed by the centralization of powerful computers, would be in harmony with prevailing needs. All private property being abolished, no kind of mortgage system would be possible either, only rentals. All services would be free. All kinds of capitalist inventorying would also become impossible if the balance of accounts (involving monetary circulation) was blocked at the level of each salary payment without any possible (monthly?) deferral. The monetary circuit serving as a vehicle of Money, operating without the generation of any surplus value and without any kind of capital accumulation, would lose the range of its toxic effects concomitant upon its role as a marker of the value of goods. The Economy would

101

orientation was, of course, vehemently disputed by the Chicago monetarists: according to these dogmatists, recession will occur in the natural course of affairs, only to be smoothed over again as equilibrium is restored between total productive expenditure, on the one hand, and real purchasing power, on the other. In which case, we don't need to do anything! So much the worse for those who suffer the consequences of this adjustment, especially as these consequences are viewed as little more than provisional. The past purportedly shows that accidents which supervene in the course of history – famines, natural evolutionary accidents, revolutions, and, of course, wars - have indeed put a block on human progress, only for the latter to resume its course in a new direction. The dogmatism of the "Chicago boys", regrettably, does not make any provision for the potential inherent in Man's anthropological heritage to control the direction of one's own affairs, decreeing conversely that State

---

thus become a more carefully considered matter, an altogether more human affair (without competition), without the violence of property vectored by Money. This scenario is, of course, a completely directorial and *dirigiste* one. Moreover, it would only be possible to envisage it after full employment had been attained. Only the power of labor would remain in order to make the Economy function (in Figure-4, only the superior plane would remain). A return to the virtuous technique of barter and exchange, along with its non-financial surpluses. It would only be possible to admit this admittedly utopian scenario if all foreign countries consented to enter into agreement with one another with a view t o practicing such a system.

intervention should be minimized at all costs. The responsibility of control is left to the system itself, which is seen to be auto-regulating thanks to the input of concerted human agency ("the invisible hand"). Ultimately, this might be construed as a kind of psychologically-driven form of self-control, with the efficiency of the system guaranteed by the concerted agency of individual 'private sector' actors. The incentive to gain[31] thus becomes the primary and superordinate motor of all economic activity.

Nevertheless, a *laisser faire* approach to the economic affairs of any given country cannot be easily deduced from all this. When it comes to the workings of an economic system, preventive direction and adjustment remain essential prerequisites in order to forestall recession and develop harmoniously as a nation. Indeed, another kind of monetarism might be possible if one were able to control monetary flows in the way that we have advocated in this essay. America is, above all, one vast enterprise. Its people willingly accept both the advantages and the drawbacks of this way of operating, both politically and economically.

---

31 This dogmatism has been formalized under the name of 'The Washington Consensus', appealing to the universality of private property and minimal state intervention. However, this doctrine has been severely called into doubt with the train of recent events, exemplified by the 'Sub-Prime crisis' involving a massive injection of new liquidity by the Federal Bank into the system, this occurring under the direct aegis of Washington.

"Indeed, it was the time when wealthy countries, bristling with new industry, brim with new shops, discovered a new kind of faith, a project at last worthy of the efforts consecrated by Man over thousands of years: to make of the world one vast and unique enterprise"[32].

The role of the State, in as much as it might once again become master of the banks, should be to diminish the predatory effects of the system as far as possible by adopting, for example, a selective tax regime or an incentive-based pricing policy (as occurred in France in the automobile sector with the *bonus-malus* system). The State might also control how much financial currency would be allowed to filter into general monetary circulation. It would do this by filtering these influxes according to their origins and their destination (loans or purchases pertaining to which range of goods? made for whom, and with what intentions?). In this way, one might hope to avoid the kind of crises that we saw in the case of the 'sub-prime' fiasco in 2007-8. Conversely, obliging banks and private companies to inject liquidity into a system of monetary circulation that is losing impetus to the detriment of growth would serve to re-orientate the whole economic system beneficially in the long term. This kind of regulation would constitute a temperate monetarism orientated toward growth; a tempered monetarism in direct contrast to the kind of free-for-all variety

32 Translation of a quote taken from *L'imrécateur* by René-Victor Pilhès, Paris, Editions de Seuil.

which has latterly unleashed so many well-publicized acts of predatory speculation, bringing in its wake untold human suffering and mounting suicide rates provoked by unemployment and recession. By following such policies, Western leaders would strike out on a wholly different tack to that advocated by the 'Washington Consensus' and the 'Boys from the Chicago School', those apostles of minimal state intervention who have been quite happy to see the predatory effects of uncontrolled speculation unleashed on a global scale. In this way, we might begin to prepare the groundwork for a renewal of prosperity and full employment, without which the well-being of the world's populations as a whole cannot be assured.

We are thus promoting a conception of Money seen as a lever of Growth and not as a predatory organ. This conception applies as much to the financial as the productive sector in as much as the former remains a necessity within a globalized economic system. Indeed, in what possible sense would the hyper-activity of economic growth be beneficial to the evolution and progress of humanity if were to destroy, rather than to consolidate, an integral part of Man's evolutionary heritage along with his vital resources?

Epilogue

The law of systems, with all of its various advantages and drawbacks, represents a universal empirical law which can be derived from the first and second principles of thermodynamics, these being themselves derived from the theory of the 'Big Bang' modeling the creation of the Universe (see Box-1).

In particular, we have been able to note that it is not possible to modify an actively functioning system from within (see Box-2). Rather, the trajectory of that which has been conceived at the origin of the system is only modifiable when confronted with external forces. At the end of the day, nothing is less intelligent than a tool. All that really counts are the intentions embodied in programs designed by Man, who, by observing the use which is made of these designs, can eventually modify them, albeit from the outside: all that needs to be done is to alter the parameters which make them function.

Since its very creation, Money has afforded Man the opportunity to make tangible material progress at a speed which has become truly extraordinary for what has been a number of centuries now. Unfortunately, the capitalist system which it generated has also brought about a number of the predatory distortions which have been so deleterious to the interests of a large part of humanity. Abolishing the predatory capitalism which has been spawned in the wake of some of the more nefarious consequences of Money could only be brought about, of course, at the price of a significant slow-down in the rate of material progress[33].

---

33 The desire to emulate which is spawned by competition in greed, both on an individual and company scale, represents a

However, even in the absence of such an ultimate and hitherto unknown reverse, one might still envisage the possibility of correcting these predatory distortions **through external intervention** as soon as they appear. As we have seen, the power of capitalism originally issued from time saved within the production process thanks to the man-made device of Money.

This remains one of its essential parameters, a motor of its very power. By exploiting this essential constituent, it would surely become possible to control the volumes of financial flows, and where they finally end up. This might be done by making a clear denominational distinction between the currencies circulating within different systems (for example, the *Ecu* for financial flows) according to their characteristics, origins and objectives.

The establishment of such a system would enable material progress to be maintained, at a lower rate certainly, but without incurring any of the drawbacks involved in the runaway rate of expansion encouraged in today's markets. It will, of course, be important not to slow these markets down too much, these being driven by productive flows which require, not stanching, but only a little redirection toward more equitable ends for the population as a whole. Similarly, energy resources might be preserved by means of a qualitative control

---

major argument for the proponents of the liberal system.

rendered visible and transparent by virtue of its separation from financial flows.

Social Man should thus, all things taken into consideration, have the means at his disposal to intervene in any given system of which he is the designer with a view to controlling and correcting any of its deviations or unwanted side-effects. Such correction might notably be brought to bear in order to rectify the present ultra-liberal thrust of the French economy, this having been initiated in the 1970's[34] and then extended in 1983 in the direction of a rigorous set of accounting procedures. These procedures were, of course, more than compatible with the predatory speculative practices coming into vogue at the time, bearing principally upon uncontrolled productive flows. Should we just stand by and let all this take its natural course[35]? Should

---

34 The tenets of this doctrine have in part been refuted by the frequent intervention which has occurred in a number of different states in order to regulate and control the present crisis. This intervention has been most palpably manifest the form of bank nationalization and in the massive aid conferred upon other ailing banks who nevertheless remained partly or wholly private (case histories abound in the U.S.A., the U.K. and France).

35 It will, of course, be necessary to invert the premises of the present system; carefully targeted Fordism will need to be established in order to generate a significant financial dynamism within the monetary circuit. This will need to be established without undue concern for any deficits which might eventually accrue. These will eventually be balanced out by the automatic yield of monetary investments.. Accordingly, the resurgence of employment and growth will be seen to be all the more rapid. Indeed, these deficits will be

we just wait in hopeful expectation for better days to come, or perhaps some kind of major social upheaval? According to the analysis of Edgar Morin, the latter may well be an inevitable consequence of what we have been analyzing, brought to pass through an ineluctable dialectic of organization, disorganization, and organization. Is he right? If he is, what kind of organization are we referring to? Would it be a democratic one? Or perhaps a highly directorial one, *ultra-dirigiste* and thus effectively dictatorial? Alternatively, will we be able to take things in hand before such a major upheaval of the existing order becomes inevitable? A wise steering of the ship before any final tumultuous shipwreck occurs is indeed what those of a present-day Keynesian persuasion hope will take place. Let us place our trust in these skilled proponents of a humanist Economy[36].

---

either ignored in the process of monetary creation or financed by borrowing from the banks (on condition, that is, that interest rates should be appropriately regulated). Alternatively, another measure which might be introduced is that of large state-financed loans distributed in a finely targeted way. Individual states would retain the theoretical power of intervention, provided that they do not become too closely bound by contervailing economic decisions imposed by the European Union. Similarly, the influence of the financial and industrial management lobbies would need to be resisted. These policies might be consolidated, if need be, by nationalizing the large banks.

36 A tradition exemplified in the works of writers such as Joseph Stiglitz, Paul Krugman (both of them Nobel Prize winners from America), Jacques Sapir, Frédéric Lordon, Paul Jorion, and many others less well-known, whose

INDEX

---

economic culture is likely to be of a more distinctly social orientation.

111